PRAISE FOR

Positive Discipline for Childcare Providers

"*Positive Discipline for Childcare Providers* is a treasure chest of effective strategies for developing the self-esteem of very young children while stimulating their 'interest in the interest of others.' In a magical way, this book demonstrates techniques that decrease misbehavior by increasing the child's sense of capability, courage, and community feeling."

—**Rob Guttenberg,** author of *The Parent as Cheerleader;* director, Parenting Education—YMCA Youth Services, Bethesda, Maryland; Maryland state certified childcare trainer

"What a wonderful tool for childcare providers! The paradigm shift in *Positive Discipline for Childcare Providers* is exactly what our country needs to improve the quality of childcare. This process offers encouragement to those professionals who are often underpaid and underappreciated. As a trainer of childcare providers, it is always a pleasure to observe those "light bulb" moments when providers realize what an important job they have and how much they influence a child's ability to learn, develop, and grow. As a parent, I would make sure my children's provider had a copy of this book."

—**Deborah Cashen,** Creating Capable Communities, Houston, Texas

"This is a superbly useful book. It is both very practical and intellectually stimulating. It offers creative—and extremely practical—solutions to difficulties commonly encountered in childcare settings. The solutions are based on an extremely valuable and useful theory that helps adults understand children and the reason why children behave (and misbehave) as they do."

—**Edward G. Abelson,** Ph.D., licensed psychologist, Ithaca, New York

"What an invaluable contribution to the childcare community. This is especially useful to new teachers who too often have to learn things the hard way through experience (sometimes with devastating effects). I can see this being used as we train our classroom assistants as well. Jane and Cheryl have a great ability to get complex ideas communicated in clear, straightforward English for all to understand. The authors give providers concrete examples and direct application of psychological theories. This hands-on book is a useful tool for the child care provider."

—**Pam Boudreau**, the Montessori School

"Wow! This book is sure to be an incredible resource in any childcare setting. It's full of effective and practical ideas—from creating an environment where everyone feels welcome to a model of discipline that respects and empowers adults and children. The topics for teachers and parents, for everything from anger to clinginess, are a nice bonus."

—**Mary Jamin Maguire**, M.A., L.P., L.I.C.S.W., trainer,
Minnesota School-Age Childcare Training Network

"This is an outstanding book! I especially love the way the authors have incorporated child development concepts and developmentally appropriate practice into all aspects of positive discipline. I recommend this book to every family childcare provider, preschool teacher and childcare teacher. The authors have succeeded in creating a practical and much-needed handbook to deal with discipline issues in early childhood education and childcare settings."

—**Kathryn Adams**, MS, assistant professor, Child Development,
San Bernardino Valley College

"This book is wonderful. It has brought more joy into my job by providing a basic review of age-appropriate behavior and child development concepts and by reminding me to focus on the innate goodness of children. I absolutely love the positive ways to deal with discipline. The information and skills I learned from this book have made me proud to be a childcare provider."

—**Rina Orme**, childcare provider, West Jordan, Utah

Positive Discipline for Childcare Providers

ALSO IN THE
POSITIVE DISCIPLINE SERIES

Jane Nelsen, Ed.D, and Cheryl Erwin, M.A.

Positive Discipline

FOR CHILDCARE PROVIDERS

A Practical and

Effective Plan for Every

Preschool and Daycare Program

THREE RIVERS PRESS · NEW YORK

Published in the United States by Three Rivers Press, an imprint of the Crown Publishing Group,
a division of Random House, Inc., New York.
www.crownpublishing.com

Three Rivers Press and the Tugboat design are registered trademarks of Random House, Inc.

Originally published in the United States by Prima Publishing, Roseville, California, in 2002.

Illustrations by Paula Gray

Library of Congress Cataloging-in-Publication Data
Nelsen, Jane.
    Positive discipline for childcare providers : a practical effective plan for every preschool and daycare
program / Jane Nelsen, Cheryl Erwin.
        p.   cm. — (Positive discipline)
    Includes index.
    ISBN 0-7615-3567-5
    1. Day care centers—United States. 2. Discipline of children—United States. I. Erwin, Cheryl.
II. Title. III. Series
HQ778.63 .N44-5   2002
362.71'2'0973—dc21   2002070519

20 OPM 14
Printed in the United States of America

First Edition

CONTENTS

ACKNOWLEDGMENTS

WE FIRST BECAME convinced of the need for quality childcare providers when we needed them to care for our own young children. Fortunately, we found them and they made our lives easier and our children better because of their love and skills.

Of course, we always acknowledge Alfred Adler and Rudolf Dreikurs for their wisdom about what children need (belonging and significance) and how to provide for their needs (through understanding their world, encouragement, and nonpunitive discipline).

We have been influenced by others too numerous to remember specifically, but we are grateful for all we learned from our Early Childhood Education teachers, from childcare providers who have attended our classes, from the teachers of many wonderful workshops and lectures, from books we have read, and from the many Positive Discipline Associates who have dedicated their amazing energy to making the world a more respectful and encouraging place.

We feel honored to be published by Prima because of their quality products, and, most of all, because of their excellent staff. Jamie Miller, our remarkable acquisitions editor, is more than an editor. She is an idea person with faith in us to carry out her ideas. We appreciate her ability to wear many hats—and we especially appreciate her friend hat.

Shawn Vreeland is an editor with unparalleled patience. He is always ready to meet all our needs without frustration—or at least none that shows.

We love the way Paula Gray is able to capture moods with her art. Her illustrations are truly worth a thousand words.

Most of all, we want to acknowledge all those who have picked up this book because they want to learn more about the children in their care. Childcare is, all too often, a thankless and unappreciated task. We acknowledge all those who spend their days in the company of children, teaching, loving, caring, and giving. Thank you.

The Fundamentals of Childcare

1

Quality Care—For You and the Children

A GREAT DEAL has been written about childcare over the past decade or two. The debate continues: Is it good or bad? What makes "quality childcare"? Does being in childcare harm children? Some people claim parents should always stay home with their growing children, that working mothers damage the children they say they love. Others claim just as loudly that childcare is beneficial to children, that childcare actually improves a child's ability to learn, develop, and grow.

As with most things in the world of human behavior, childcare is not a simple proposition; much of its value (or potential to cause harm) depends on the way it is provided and structured. But whatever form it may take, childcare is here to stay for millions of working parents and their families. In every community across this nation, there are scores of childcare options. And some parents agonize over the selection of a care facility or provider. They search long and hard to find just the "right" place, and each morning they drop their child off and drive away, enduring the apprehension that comes with leaving the child they love in the hands of someone else. Parents feel both anxiety and a compelling desire to trust their caregiver, whether that caregiver is part of a large childcare center or someone who cares for children in his or her home, a trained early childhood educator and child development specialist, or an old-fashioned babysitter.

One thing is clear: While high-quality care may indeed benefit children,[1] mediocre or substandard care certainly can be harmful, and some parents don't take the time or possess the knowledge to find quality child care.

> Childcare is not a simple proposition; much of its value (or potential to cause harm) depends on the way it is provided and structured.

Our purpose in writing this book is to help those who care for and work with young children create an environment where those children can thrive, where they can learn, laugh, and grow, and where their healthy development—physical, emotional, and cognitive—is supported and encouraged. We will explore child development, brain growth, temperament, and age-appropriate behavior; we will also look at ways you can work with children who may have special needs. We will discover ways you can create a facility that is inviting and nurturing for children and encouraging for the adults who work there, and find ways to partner with parents (who sometimes may seem like more of a challenge than their children). And we will help you deal with that most difficult challenge of all—discipline. Finding a way to meet all these important needs is what creates quality childcare.

Quality Care Defined

WHAT IS QUALITY care, and how do you provide it for yourself and for children? We believe that "quality care" means providing an environment where everyone (including you, your staff and coworkers, and the children you care for) feels nurtured and supported, able to grow and blossom to his or her full potential.

In a nurturing environment, people feel a sense of belonging and significance. They feel capable and know they can make a positive difference in their community (large or small). They have many opportunities to learn valuable life skills and to use mistakes as wonderful opportunities for learning. In a quality care environment, people are treated with dignity and respect, no mat-

---

1. NICHD Early Child Care Research Network, "Characteristics of Infant Child Care: Factors Contributing to Positive Caregiving," *Early Childhood Research Quarterly* 11 (1996): 269–306.

ter what happens during the day. They also feel safe—both physically and emotionally.

Quality childcare provides a stimulating environment that values the importance of play for children five and under and does not push academics that may only frustrate children and give them a sense of inadequacy. Adults providing quality care have taken the time to understand child development concepts, age appropriateness, and brain development research; they do not have expectations that are beyond the capability of children to fulfill. They know how to differentiate between the kind of discipline that is discouraging to children and the kind of discipline that is empowering to children—and there is a difference.[2]

Quality care" means providing an environment where everyone (including you, your staff and coworkers, and the children you care for) feels nurtured and supported, able to grow and blossom to his or her full potential.

And don't forget about the parents. Quality childcare includes good communication with parents. Encourage parents to spend at least an hour in your home or center *with* their child so they will have a good sense of the environment they are choosing for their child. Let them know they can drop by any

2. We strongly recommend professional training in early childhood education. However, if you are unable to take classes, you can and should learn the basics of child development. This book can help, as well as these additional titles in the POSITIVE DISCIPLINE series: Jane Nelsen, Cheryl Erwin, and Roslyn Duffy, *Positive Discipline: The First Three Years* (Roseville, CA: Prima, 1998); and Jane Nelsen, Cheryl Erwin, and Roslyn Duffy, *Positive Discipline for Preschoolers*, rev. 2d ed. (Roseville, CA: Prima, 1998).

time to see how their child is doing. Yes, this may be upsetting to a small child who is still dealing with separation anxiety, but this is a small price to pay for the assurance such visits give parents. (They are unlikely to drop by any time but will feel reassured by just knowing they can.)

> At its best, childcare is a *partnership* between providers and parents; children will thrive when they experience the same kind, firm limits and respectful environment at home and at their childcare center.

Education is as good for parents as it is for you, so we have included tips and activities (in the topics section) that you can share with parents and/or your staff. Some childcare center directors like to use these activities for staff in-service trainings. Home childcare providers can give them as handouts for their parents. The activities and suggestions provide information that is useful for understanding children and how to teach, encourage, and discipline them. At its best, childcare is a *partnership* between providers and parents; children will thrive when they experience the same kind, firm limits and respectful environment at home and at their childcare center.

Throughout this book we will explore what respectful discipline and quality care looks like for children. For now, let's start with you.

Quality Care for You

QUALITY CHILDCARE, WHETHER it happens in a home or in a large center, is all but impossible unless caregivers first understand the importance of caring for themselves. You may wonder why a book on childcare would begin with the notion of caring for yourself. Well, consider Carolyn. Carolyn opened a childcare center because she loves children but has been unable to have any of her own. She spent money, time, enthusiasm, and energy educating herself, hiring the right staff, buying just the right equipment, and doing her best to create an environment that is pleasant and welcoming for the children she cares for.

Carolyn decided to start small, so she has "only" thirty children in her small building. She hired three helpers, all of whom love children but only one of whom have any formal training in child development. Their day begins at six in the morning, when they open the center and begin to receive children. Carolyn often doesn't arrive home until seven o'clock at night, after the last parent has departed and the center has been cleaned up for the next day. Then she has dinner to cook (or clean up after—she and her husband take turns) and the usual chores around the house to keep up with. She rarely crawls into bed before eleven o'clock at night. Sometimes she wonders how she'd manage if she had children of her own.

Carolyn knows her staff needs breaks during the day, but she rarely seems to find time for one herself; some days she doesn't even eat lunch. On a *really* busy day, she's lucky to make it to the bathroom. Carolyn used to enjoy running, hiking, and camping with her husband, but these days her weekends are filled with trainings and workshops. She pores over resource materials looking for new programs and ideas. She buys supplies and prepares for the week ahead. Her husband grumbles, and Carolyn does her best to pretend she isn't exhausted. She begins to dread the beginning of each day, to complain about her staff, and to snap at the children when they don't behave the way she wants them to. She resents the parents who never understand how hard her job is and who are often slow to pay for childcare and late to pick up their children. Carolyn begins to wonder why she ever thought the childcare center was such a great idea.

Carolyn desperately needs to learn to take care of herself, to balance the work she loves with her own emotional and physical health. But she feels guilty when she takes time to relax, especially when there is always something waiting to be

done. The truth is that taking time for *you* is not selfish. It is the best thing you can do for your family, your own children (if you have them), and the children you care for. You have to fill your own cup before you have anything to give.

One of the primary reasons people decide to provide childcare in their own homes is because they have children of their own and do not want to leave them to work outside the home. Another reason is that they really like children. (We are sure this doesn't need to be said to anyone who cares enough to read this book, but we will say it anyway just to make a very strong statement: If you don't like children, stop being a childcare provider immediately. We can't imagine anything more harmful for children than having to spend hours each day with someone who doesn't like them.)

> You have to fill your own cup before you have anything to give.

So, when you start out with such noble reasons—to be with your own children and because you like children—what can go wrong? Lots! Like Carolyn, you can forget to take care of yourself and get too tired. You can become overwhelmed with the challenges of being on call for needy children without a break and having to deal with children who can be obnoxious at times. As one childcare provider said, "Sometimes I have to take a deep breath and remind myself that I really like children. Then I call my sister-in-law, who is also a childcare provider, and we give each other support. She reassures me that I'm normal to feel overwhelmed at times and to sometimes feel I don't like these children. Just feeling understood is like a breath of fresh air and I feel nurtured and ready to nurture again."

Create a Support System

If you don't have a friend who is in the childcare business, find one. Call your local childcare referral agency (available in most cities) and get the names of other childcare providers. Call them up and invite them to be part of a phone support system.

If you are taking early childhood education classes (more about that later), be on the lookout for people whose company you enjoy. Get their phone numbers and agree to give each other support, both for emotional comfort and for sharing ideas. Early childhood education conferences and workshops (local, state, and national) are great for ideas and networking.

If you have access to the Internet, there is an amazing amount of information available. A good place to start is the National Child Care Information Center (www.nccic.org). This group has enough links to keep you busy for a long time. The Child Care Parent Provider Information Network (www.childcare-ppin .com) has chat rooms where you can chat with other childcare providers.

> If you don't have a friend who is in the childcare business, find one.

Let Your Children Be a Part of Your Support System

If you care for children in your own home, you may have noticed that your own children usually have opinions and reactions to their temporary siblings. Some childcare providers feel guilty because their own children have to share them with the children they provide care for. Others feel they may be "too hard" on their own children by making them conform to what they expect of other children—or by making them share their toys and personal belongings. (A problem that, incidentally, is shared by childcare center staff whose own children attend the center where they work.) Whatever the reasons, to compensate for their guilt, they make the mistake of pampering their children after the other children go home, or feel they shouldn't expect too much from them.

Remember, though, that children love to help. Your children may cooperate and feel more comfortable with the childcare environment when they are

respectfully involved in the process of helping. (They *don't* like being ordered around at the whim of their parents or teachers.)

Let your children help you plan for the following day. They can help you set out materials and make lunches. Let them decide what toys they would like to put away and not share. (For more examples, see the story about Sandy on page 110.) Ask them for suggestions about how to encourage a child you care for who may be misbehaving because he feels discouraged. (See chapter 3 for more information regarding "a misbehaving child is a discouraged child.") This can teach them compassion and give them the joy of knowing they can help others.

> Your children may cooperate and feel more comfortable with the childcare environment when they are respectfully involved in the process of helping.

Children can offer support and cooperation no matter where you care for them. If you work in a large center, you can still find ways to involve and invite children in helping, making a contribution, and feeling like a significant and welcome part of their childcare experience (rather than a burden). You will learn more about involving children in the chapters ahead.

Plan in Advance

Regardless of where you work, a very important part of taking care of you is to nurture the time you have with your own family. In our busy, hectic world, this takes some planning.

Have you ever noticed that it takes more energy to *think* about what to cook for dinner than it does to actually *cook* the dinner? There are a number of ways to ease the pressure of feeding your family at the end of a tiring day. You can get your older children involved (during a weekend family meeting) in planning all the meals for the week. (They will gain a sense of belonging and significance, as well as useful life skills.) Cook double batches of food on weekends so you will have delicious leftovers during the week when you are tired.

Plan for fun times with your family. It doesn't help to say "someday." During a family meeting, brainstorm all the fun things (those that are free and those that cost money) that you would like to do as a family. Then choose as many things as you can and put them on the calendar.

Plan for special time with each of your own children. Special planned time is in addition to all the regular time you spend interacting with your child and can take as little as ten minutes a day for children five years old and younger. Then, when they make demands when you really don't have time, you can say, "I don't have time now, but I sure am looking forward to our special time at seven o'clock." This statement is often enough to soothe demanding children because they don't get the sense that they are being neglected—at least, not forever.

School-aged children will appreciate thirty minutes of planned special time once a week, time that is just theirs to play a game or do a special project together. Teenagers may lose interest in spending time with you, but you can still insist that a date night once a month (for pizza, a movie, or a shopping trip) is very important to you—and that you won't tell their friends that they are spending time with you.

> Special planned time can take as little as ten minutes a day for children five years old and younger.

Find Time for Yourself

Finding time for yourself can seem almost impossible for a person trying to juggle family and childcare. However, it is essential for you to fill your cup; you cannot give to others what you do not have yourself. If you are a morning person, get up twenty to thirty minutes earlier than you "have" to so you can

sit by yourself and enjoy any activity that energizes, refreshes, or feels good to you. You may need to go to bed a little earlier so you can get enough sleep. If you are a night person, you will prefer to find your personal special time after your children go to bed. You can kindly but firmly let your family know that this part of each day belongs to you.

We encourage you to make special time for yourself part of every day. You may choose to curl up with a good book, take a bubble bath with candles, work out at a gym, listen to music, practice yoga, or talk to a friend over a cup of tea.

> People who have begun spending twenty to thirty minutes of self-care time daily can tell you how much more energy they have for giving when they have had some time just for themselves.

You may be surprised at the results; people who have begun spending twenty to thirty minutes of self-care time daily can tell you how much more energy they have for giving when they have had some time just for themselves. Another way to spend time for yourself is to continue your education.

Continue Your Education

Formal education is not required to be a childcare provider, but it is an excellent way to care for yourself and to enhance your effectiveness in your career. Continuing your education does not have to be overwhelming. You can enroll in a community college and take just one class a semester in early childhood education. Many states provide incentives (money) to encourage continuing education for childcare providers.

The benefits of early childhood education classes are that you will learn things that will make your job easier. You will increase your understanding of child development and age appropriateness. Curriculum classes will provide you with hundreds of ideas you can use with the children you care for—ideas that will make your job easier. And continuing to educate yourself will give you more professionalism and pride in what you do.

Value Yourself and What You Do

What is the most important job in the world? We have no doubt that it is caring for children. Sadly, it is also among the lowest-paying jobs. Don't let low pay influence the importance you attach to what you do. Be proud of what you do and the difference you can make in the lives of children—who are, after all, the future of our world. You wouldn't be reading this book if you were not interested in learning all you can to improve yourself and your skills—and thus your positive influence on children. So stand tall, and do all you can to provide quality care for children.

Quality Care for Children

BECAUSE A MAJOR portion of this book focuses on quality care (nurturing) through Positive Discipline methods, in this chapter we will cover the importance of a nurturing physical environment and a nurturing routine for quality childcare. Some

> Formal education is not required to be a childcare provider, but it is an excellent way to care for yourself and to enhance your effectiveness in your career.

of the suggestions are obvious and probably are things you are already doing. We hope that you will find some new ideas that will be helpful and will increase your effectiveness. This example focuses on Julie, who provides childcare in her own home, but you will find ideas that are easy to transfer to even the largest center.

Physical Environment

When Julie decided to become a childcare provider, she looked at the living room that she hadn't been able to afford to furnish and thought, "What a great place for childcare! I can earn some money instead of worrying that I don't have enough to spend." She issued a challenge to herself to furnish the room as well and as inexpensively as possible.

Julie found a used flat door. Her husband put short legs on it and she painted it bright red. She found ten plastic chairs at a "dollar store" for a dollar each. Ten children (her limit) fit just fine around this inexpensive table, which is perfect for art projects, play dough, snacks, and lunch.

Julie and her husband built shelves out of boards and cinder blocks for toys on one wall and hung low hooks on another wall for coats and higher hooks for toy bags. Julie had the great idea to make drawstring bags for blocks and other toys that came in pieces. The children have to put one set of toys in a bag

TAKING CARE OF YOURSELF

Providing care for others begins with taking good care of yourself. Here are some ideas to consider:

- Create a support system.
- Let your children be a part of your support system.
- Plan in advance.
- Find time for yourself.
- Continue your education.
- Value yourself and what you do.

before they can have another one. (Children will get every toy off the shelf before putting anything away if they have a chance. Cleaning up is much less overwhelming—for you and for them—when you help them learn to pick up one set before getting another.)

One corner of the room was saved for children to stack their sleeping bags (brought from home and sent home once a week for washing) for quiet time. (We are careful not to call it "nap time," and you should be, too. See Nap Time in the topics section for more information.) In another corner there was room for a box of dress-up clothes. The toy shelves were filled with wooden puzzles, books, and some sturdy Tonka trucks and Fisher-Price toys they had found at Goodwill (and scrubbed clean with lots of Lysol). Clothesline was strung from one corner of the room to another with lots of clothespins for hanging the children's artwork.

Julie got very creative in her fenced-in yard. She found an old oil drum and painted it red to look like the front of a train engine. She put it on a small platform and fastened four old tires along the sides. Her husband found some used lumber and built a tall platform with railings behind the oil drum. It includes a ladder the kids use to climb up to the platform. On one side he built a rope ladder that the kids can climb on. They built a sand pile underneath the platform with lots of sand toys. They also had a regular swing and slide set, but the "choo-choo train" invites lots of creative play. Julie was now ready for the children.

Routines

Routines are very important to give children a sense of order and security. The following routine is just one possibility. Depending on the ages of your children, you may need to eliminate some of the suggestions and/or rearrange the order to suit your needs.

Julie starts with a breakfast of orange juice and cold cereal. Some of the kids have already eaten, and some have not. Even those who have eaten seem to enjoy pouring their own cereal and milk from small containers.

Breakfast is followed by free play because the children arrive at different times. Julie always invites two children to help her get the art project ready. They take turns according to the "Helpers Chart." We have included recipes for many art projects (see appendix A). Following are three of Julie's favorites:

- **Junk art:** (See glue recipe in appendix A.) This is the children's favorite, so they often do junk art two or three times a week. Julie saves (and asks the children's parents to save) all kinds of things for junk art: macaroni, leaves, pebbles, sticks, paper clips, yarn, beads from broken jewelry, cut up pieces of material, colored paper, and so on. The "junk" is spread out in the center of the table. Each child receives a piece of construction paper and a used butter tub containing the homemade glue. They choose pieces of junk and glue it on the construction paper.

> Routines are very important to give children a sense of order and security.

- **Play dough:** (See recipe in appendix A.) Children love playing with homemade play dough. They can pound, roll, or actually make shapes. It is easy and cheap to make.

- **Finger paint:** (See recipe in appendix A.) Julie regularly gets an end roll of newsprint from her local newspaper. Newsprint paper is great for finger painting. (Some children don't want to get "messy" by using the finger paint. Have crayons available for them, as well as old shirts to cover clothing.)

Outside play (weather permitting) occurs after the children help Julie clean up the art table. They love working with water and sponges to clean up—after time for training on how to squeeze the sponges after dipping them in the clean water bucket before wiping up the table, and then squeezing again in the dirty water bucket before going to the clean water bucket again. (For information on teaching life skills to children, see chapter 3.)

Julie uses circle time as the time for songs, finger plays, story time, and maybe a theme such as colors or shapes. You may have children of different ages, which can make it difficult to meet the needs of every child. Most children enjoy songs and finger plays, but it is best not to force those who don't want to participate. Some children may be fully engaged, while others prefer to wander and have free play.

Lunch is an important part of everyone's day. Some childcare providers ask the parents to bring their child's lunch. Others fix lunch so all children will have the same thing. Julie prefers to have sandwich fixings (turkey slices, peanut butter, lettuce, mayonnaise, mustard, jelly) on hand and let children make their own sandwiches. She and the older children help the younger children in preparing lunch and setting the table.

> Most children enjoy songs and finger plays, but it is best not to force those who don't want to participate.

Quiet time is required for young children in many communities, but Julie has discovered that trying to make children take a nap is a never-ending battle. She simply makes it clear that children don't have to sleep but need to rest quietly. If they want to read a book while lying on their mat or sleeping bag, that is fine. Julie has found it helpful to have soft music playing. Younger children will probably fall asleep. Children who are four and five years old (and who have outgrown napping) might sit at a kitchen table doing a quiet project or do something else that is quiet and doesn't disturb children who are likely to sleep. Sometimes Julie uses this time to engage older children in a class meeting to let them practice compliments and work on solutions to problems that might be on the agenda. (See pages 54–58.)

Quiet time is followed by free play (outside or in) until parents come—usually at different times. Parents seem to appreciate it when Julie takes a few moments to talk with them about their child's day.

We have already discussed the benefits to children of routines. Parents will also appreciate knowing what their child's day will be like, so Julie posts a routine chart in a conspicuous place. Using a Polaroid or digital camera, she also likes to include pictures of children doing the tasks listed on the chart.

Julie has found that posting the routine chart serves two purposes. First, both parents and children can see the routine chart and have a handy "map" for the day's activities. Second, she can let the children tell her what is next on the routine chart (this is especially useful when they get distracted or "off task"). Letting the children check the chart increases cooperation and allows the routine to become the "boss."

Turn Off the TV

You'll notice that television is not mentioned in any of the routines at Julie's center. We agree with her approach and strongly suggest that television not be part of the child's day. The research is clear that screen time can be harmful to healthy brain development (see chapter 4). A sure way to identify poor-quality childcare is an environment where children are planted in front of the television instead of engaging in activities or where television is substituted for life skills, active play, and opportunities for real learning.

> We strongly suggest that television not be part of the child's day.

THIRTEEN TIPS FOR CLASSROOM SUCCESS

Sometimes the simplest suggestions make the biggest difference in your childcare day.

Keep the following tips in mind when working with the children in your care:

1. Learn and use the children's names. Make eye contact whenever possible.

2. Be alert. Move around whenever you are needed. Give guidance as needed, but try not to interfere in a child's activities unless there is a distinct need (i.e., the child is in danger or is endangering another).

3. Be willing to act. Standing and watching are not as helpful as action; if your specific duty is to put out playground equipment and a jar of paint is spilled, pitch in and help the person in charge of art clean it up.

4. Each teacher should always have a full view of the classroom. The teacher's back should never be turned toward the majority of the children.

5. Young children can and should do many things for themselves. Encourage them to do things independently and to reason things out for themselves. Do not answer a question if it is possible for you to help the child think of the answer through "what" and "how" questions. When possible, give the child suggestions for "doing" rather than "doing for" the child. Help only when the child really needs help.

6. Avoid excess chatter about the children with other teachers while in the classroom. Teacher attention needs to be on the children, not talking about them, their parents, other staff, and so on.

7. Be consistent. Children should know that certain results will always follow a given action. Be warm and kind, but firm when necessary. Physical

punishment, sarcasm, or any type of correction that is humiliating or embarrassing to children is unacceptable.

8. Know where supplies and equipment are kept. Keep things organized but do not make clean-up a burdensome, constant task for children. Children should be encouraged but not forced to participate in clean-up.

9. If a child wets or soils his or her clothing, show no shock; do not embarrass the child.

10. Children should be free to use materials as they wish, as long as they use them appropriately. Children enjoy having teachers sit with them when they are doing an activity. However, teachers should use wisdom in displaying things they have made because children may become frustrated when their own creation does not look the same.

11. Every child does not have to participate in a group activity, but when a child is in the group, he or she should be attentive. At least one alternative activity should be going on for those who are not participating in the group activity. Those not involved in the group should not be allowed to disturb those who are.

12. Watch for opportunities to work with a child individually. During free play, work with a child on a puzzle, read to a child, and so on.

13. Respect children's feelings and decisions. A child may not do as you ask or fail to respond to you for many reasons. Try not to take it personally. Laugh with children but never at them. Do your best to keep your facial expression and your voice pleasant. Enjoy the children; they are wonderful, fascinating people.

(Courtesy of Rebecca Carter-Steele, Campus Childcare Connections, University of Nevada, Reno.)

Perfection "Not"

SO, YOU HAVE provided quality care for yourself and a quality environment and routine for the children in your care. Does this mean everything will always go smoothly? We *wish* (and we bet you do, too). However, as you already know, that just isn't the way it is. Children will get discouraged and will misbehave. You will get discouraged and question that this is the most important job in the world. Just remember that no matter what you have chosen to do with your time, life will always have its ups and downs. Hopefully this book will help you get through the downs and provide you with information, ideas, and resources so you will experience more ups and can continue to provide quality care for children.

2

Dispelling the Myths
About Discipline

ONE OF THE reasons caregivers and parents buy books about children is to learn about discipline. In fact, learning more about discipline and "classroom management" may be the reason you are reading this book right now. But what *is* effective discipline? Are there any magic tools to make children behave? What can you do with a room full of noisy, active, independent youngsters? Well, we intend to challenge your thinking about discipline. (Maybe you understand the true purpose of discipline but will be grateful that others are challenged.) Conventional wisdom about discipline (those ideas held by the majority of people) is filled with myths and mistakes about what discipline means, what it should look like, and what kind of discipline is effective to motivate positive change in children.

Think for a minute. What do most people think discipline means? What discipline methods are most popular in homes and schools today? How many adults still believe that a "good spanking" is sometimes necessary? Most "discipline" methods actually fall under the heading of punishment. The

Conventional wisdom about discipline (those ideas held by the majority of people) is filled with myths and mistakes about what discipline means, what it should look like, and what kind of discipline is effective to motivate positive change in children.

following is a list of what we hear when parents and teachers tell us they have "tried everything":

- Time-out, grounding, suspension, or isolation
- Withdrawal of privileges
- Lectures
- Nagging
- Threats (sometimes called "warnings"), counting to three
- Spanking, slapping, paddling, ear pinching
- Shaming, guilt, name-calling ("bad boy, bad girl")
- Public humiliation (standing "on the wall," moving cards or colors on a classroom board, wearing a fanny-pack with tickets that must be handed to a teacher for every infraction, and other forms of "discipline" that happen in the presence of a child's peers)

Other "discipline" methods fall under the heading of rewards:

- Money
- Food
- Stars, stickers, tickets, smiley faces
- Promises
- Praise
- Special privileges, such as lunch with the teacher only for those children who are "good" or who earn enough rewards

> The long-term results of both punishment and reward are ineffective at best and damaging at worst.

None of these methods are effective in the long term. Oh, all of them may work temporarily—punishment may stop the behavior for the moment, and rewards may motivate good behavior for a short time. However, too many adults do not consider the long-term results—and the long-term results of both punishment and reward are ineffective at best and damaging at worst.

Reams of research demonstrate that despite our historical reliance on them, punishment and rewards are ineffective and/or harmful, especially when the long-term results are considered.[1] So why do thousands of parents and teachers still use these archaic methods?

- They don't know better because the research is buried in academic journals.

- Punishment and rewards are myths (sins) that have been passed on from generation to generation.

- Punishment and rewards are familiar, require little thought or planning, and are easy to apply when challenged. In fact, they are often applied as knee-jerk reactions.

> Praise and rewards are actually discouraging to children, reducing their motivation to learn and cooperate.

- People are deceived because punishment and rewards do work in the short term, even though long-term results are negative.

- Punishment and rewards give adults a sense of power and control, and they temporarily alleviate their sense of anger or annoyance.

Many teachers and caregivers can accept that punishment may not be a good idea but believe that rewards—a little "incentive"—are fine. They mistakenly believe that the way to encourage and help children feel better is through praise and material rewards. Surprisingly, however, praise and rewards are actually discouraging to children, reducing their motivation to learn and cooperate.

Rewards teach children to respond to an "external locus of control." In other words, they learn to do things for the reward only. This makes the adult responsible—not the children. It is the adult's job to catch kids when they are "good" so they can dole out rewards and to catch kids being "bad" so they can mete out the punishment. But what happens when the adult is not around?

---

1. For more information and research on this important subject, see Alfie Kohn's excellent book *Punished by Rewards* (Boston: Houghton Mifflin, 1999); Jane Nelsen and Cheryl Erwin, *Parents Who Love Too Much: How Good Parents Can Learn to Love More Wisely and Develop Children of Character* (Roseville, CA: Prima, 2000); or Jane Nelsen, Cheryl Erwin, and Roslyn Duffy, *Positive Discipline for Preschoolers*, rev. 2d ed. (Roseville, CA: Prima, 1998).

One of the primary principles of Positive Discipline is to teach children to do the right thing for the intrinsic feeling of goodness for doing the deed and to make a contribution to society. Conventional wisdom teaches that rewards are the best motivators to help children do better. Indeed, many children will be motivated by rewards for a while. However, have you noticed that they soon want bigger rewards? Other children attempt to negotiate a better deal each time around or they eventually refuse to do the task at all. We feel certain you would rather spend time with children who have learned self-discipline rather than children who depend on you for rewards or punishment.

A Paradigm Shift

WE'VE EXPLORED WHAT true discipline is *not*, but what *is* it? The word *discipline* comes from the same Latin root *(discipulus)* as the word *disciple* and has much the same meaning: to teach or to follow a venerated leader. Wouldn't it be lovely to have the children you work with each day see you as their venerated leader?

Discipline is not at all the same thing as punishment. Punishment is something painful or humiliating that a more powerful person does to a less powerful one in the hope of producing a change in behavior. And punishment works—if all you care about is changing behavior for the moment. Sometimes, though, we must beware of what "works." Over the long term, punishment doesn't teach children what most adults think it does. As we will learn in the chapters ahead, children are always thinking, feeling, and making decisions about the people and events around them. When children are punished, their decisions often have more to do with avoiding future punishment, defying adults, or becoming a "people pleaser" than with choosing appropriate behavior.

Unfortunately, many classroom management techniques taught in universities and education programs these days rely on behavior modification or punishment and rewards. And punishment and rewards are not effective in making long-term positive changes in a child's behavior.

Change Your Vocabulary, Change Your Attitude

> Punishment and rewards are not effective in making long-term positive changes in a child's behavior.

WHAT WOULD HAPPEN if you substituted the word "teaching" for the word "discipline" in your daily work with children? Instead of searching for ways to "discipline" little Johnny when he throws a toy or pushes another child (which usually means some sort of punishment is about to happen), you might focus on finding ways to *teach* Johnny different, more respectful ways to solve his problem. Which do you think would be more effective?

While words without action change little in life, acquiring a new, more respectful vocabulary may be the first step toward acting in more respectful, effective ways and maintaining a more positive attitude. Therapists understand this principle and often spend time with their clients helping them to hear and, eventually, to change their "self-talk," the ways they speak to and about themselves. For example, telling yourself, "I made a mistake—what a great opportunity to learn!" is much more productive than muttering under your breath, "You stupid moron—you'll never get anything right."

Changing the words you use about the children in your care, their parents, your coworkers, and the ups and downs of daily life may not seem like a particularly effective discipline tool, but changing your vocabulary changes your attitude. And changing your attitude changes everything.

Here are some examples of the ways words can change attitudes—and actions:

From:	To:
"That child is difficult."	"That child is discouraged."
"Jason is so bossy!"	"Jason has real leadership qualities."
"Cassie is too stubborn!"	"Cassie certainly has perseverance!"
"That child is such a whiner."	"That child really needs some positive attention."

True discipline motivates children to cooperate, to choose appropriate behavior, and to welcome the opportunity to make a contribution to their classroom, their peers, and their families. This sort of discipline is based on teaching, on attitudes that allow adults to view children's less lovely qualities as opportunities for change and growth, and on mutual respect.

The three criteria (attitudes) for discipline that is effective are as follows:

1. Is it respectful?
2. Is it effective long term?
3. Does it teach valuable life skills for good character?

Acquiring a new, more respectful vocabulary may be the first step toward acting in more respectful, effective ways and maintaining a more positive attitude.

Is It Respectful?

Adults often assume that children should treat *them* with respect, but they haven't considered the importance of returning the favor. Teaching by example and modeling are essential for children to learn respect.

Respect is an essential element of all healthy relationships—in marriage, in the workplace, between friends, and between adults and children—and children are most likely to offer respect when it is demonstrated to them each and every day. This is why we advocate discipline tools that are kind and firm at the same time. Kindness shows respect for the child, while firmness shows respect

THREE CRITERIA FOR EFFECTIVE DISCIPLINE

1. Is it respectful?
2. Is it effective long term?
3. Does it teach valuable life skills for good character?

for the adult and for the needs of the situation. In the long term, children learn what they live.

Is It Effective Long Term?

One of the biggest reasons adults are fooled into believing that punishment works is because it does—for a short time. Children usually stop misbehavior for a while when punished. However, the long-term results usually are not effective. As we will explain in greater detail in chapter 3, children are always making decisions (subconsciously), and the decisions they make as a result of punishment usually are not the sort that will motivate them toward confidence, cooperation, and positive behavior in the future. We believe children who are punished make one of four decisions:

> Kindness shows respect for the child, while firmness shows respect for the adult and for the needs of the situation.

The Four Rs of Punishment

1. **Resentment:** "This is unfair."
2. **Rebellion:** "You can't make me. I'll do what I want."
3. **Revenge:** "You have hurt me and I'll hurt you back."
4. **Retreat:**
   a. Sneakiness: "I won't get caught next time."
   b. Low self-concept: "I'm a bad person."

Positive Discipline methods are designed to be effective long term because they are respectful and because they also teach life skills.

Does It Teach Valuable Life Skills for Good Character?

Teachers, caregivers, and parents all want children to develop healthy self-esteem. Many programs over the years have been designed to foster self-esteem in children, with varying degrees of success. We believe that there is no better way to develop self-esteem, self-respect, and confidence than teaching and practicing life skills, the real skills and abilities each of us needs to manage life, emotions, relationships, and the myriad activities of each day.

> It may seem insultingly obvious to say, but children are not born with an innate ability to manage their lives.

It may seem insultingly obvious to say, but children are not born with an innate ability to manage their lives. Tasks that seem easy to adults may be mystifying to young children, and their perception of what things mean can be amazingly different than yours. You know what you mean when you say, "Let's clean up the art table," but the process can be confusing and completely overwhelming to a preschooler.

What does discipline have to do with life skills? Well, getting children involved in finding solutions is a discipline method and a great life skill. Teaching children about positive time-out to feel better so they can do better is an excellent life skill. Teaching children to create routine charts is a time management skill they can use all their lives. These are just a few examples of discipline methods that reduce behavior problems and also teach life skills and good character. You are likely to encounter less resistance and defiance when children feel capable and competent and when they possess the knowledge, confidence, and skills to cooperate and contribute. Be sure you take time for training each time you ask a child to perform a new (or even a familiar) task. Do the task alongside the child; gradually transfer responsibility over to her.

Remember, too, that children love to imitate adults. If you get out the vacuum cleaner, you are likely to have half a dozen willing volunteers. A wise person once said that it is easier to tame a fanatic than to put life into a corpse:

Instead of telling children they are too little and sending them off to play, invite them to help you. Give them simple instructions on how a task should be done, and be sure your expectations are realistic. Then let them try and celebrate the results! Young children can usually do far more than adults think they can.

Opportunities for life skills training abound in the childcare center. With patient teaching and supervision, children can help prepare snacks and meals, clean up, organize shelves, pull weeds on the playground—the possibilities are endless. You may have a job chart with a slot for each child's name on a laminated card; you can rotate jobs each day or each week. Offering children responsibility and asking for their help can be a marvelous way to defuse poor behavior in a child who feels he doesn't

> You are likely to encounter less resistance and defiance when children feel capable and competent and when they possess the knowledge, confidence, and skills to cooperate and contribute.

belong. What better way than saying "I need your help" and teaching life skills to build a sense of belonging and significance, and to encourage self-esteem and confidence?

Learning to view discipline as teaching and finding useful, practical tools to teach children appropriate behavior takes a "paradigm shift" in thinking. But you will discover that it's well worth the effort. The next chapter on

Offering children responsibility and asking for their help can be a marvelous way to defuse poor behavior in a child who feels he doesn't belong.

basic Positive Discipline tools will help you discover specific ideas to deal with specific situations; the topics in the next section of the book will also give you ideas on how to put these principles into everyday practice. The most important thing, however, is your own attitude and approach. If you truly desire to teach and encourage your children, rather than to punish or control them, finding the best "tool" will become much easier.

3

Basic Positive Discipline Skills for Caregivers

You may have heard of Positive Discipline before; you may have attended a workshop, read one of the many Positive Discipline parenting books, or seen books that were designed to help classroom teachers work effectively with older children. But this book is special: It has been designed especially for you, someone who spends hours each day caring for other people's children. It outlines ways you can provide a healthy, safe, and encouraging atmosphere for children, parents, and staff. And it provides answers to some of the everyday challenges caregivers face in working with young children.

We have begun by defining "quality care" and exploring some of the myths and misconceptions about discipline. Now we want to build a foundation of basic Positive Discipline tools and concepts for childcare providers. With those concepts firmly in mind, you can move on to the challenges, presented in "A to Z" format, that caregivers face on a daily basis, and find ways not only to deal with them but also to prevent them in the future.

A Word About Positive Discipline

POSITIVE DISCIPLINE IS based on the work of Alfred Adler and Rudolf Dreikurs, pioneers in the field of human relationships. They believed that people do their best, work their hardest, and are happiest when they enjoy relationships built on mutual respect and dignity, encouragement, and kind, firm teaching and when they have opportunities to make a contribution to others, to cooperate, to solve problems, and to learn valuable life skills—in other words, when they feel encouraged.

"Wait a minute," you may be thinking. "Those ideas sound great for grown-ups or teenagers, but what toddlers and young children need is discipline. They need structure and supervision. And surely you can't mean that three-year-olds will cooperate and solve problems!"

Well, maybe not all the time; after all, two- and three-year-olds are firmly entrenched in a developmental stage that urges them to explore their own initiative and autonomy. (We will take a closer look at development in chapter 4.) Preschoolers do not see the world as adults do. They do not have equal rights with adults (for good reason), and they do not have exactly the same needs, but they *do* have equal worth as human beings. Like adults, they will do their best when they experience a sense of belonging and significance, when their developmental needs and abilities are understood, and when they receive kind, firm discipline that teaches, rather than punishment or rewards that manipulate, shame, or discourage.

> Preschoolers will do their best when they experience a sense of belonging and significance, when their developmental needs and abilities are understood, and when they receive kind, firm discipline that teaches, rather than punishment or rewards that manipulate, shame, or discourage.

Understanding the concepts of Positive Discipline will help you create a warm, encouraging, enjoyable place for children to come and stay, a place where children, parents, and caregivers can feel safe, respected, and involved. You will learn positive strategies to deal with misbehavior—strategies that are based first on understanding the child and second on ways that encourage the development of valuable life skills. Let's explore the basic tools of Positive Discipline.

The Primary Human Need

ASK MOST PARENTS and teachers what children need to be healthy, secure, and happy, and they have a simple answer: love. Love certainly is important for

parents and their children, but what about teachers and caregivers, who are unlikely to really *love* each child they care for? You may not *love* each child, but it is essential that you show respect and caring for each child. (More about this later in this chapter.) Actually, what children (and, for that matter, teenagers and adults) really need is what we call *a sense of belonging and significance.* Love is only part of belonging. It is just as important to feel capable and to develop the skills for making a meaningful contribution in your world. Children feel belonging and significance when they are taught to use their power and autonomy in useful ways instead of for "power struggles." They feel belonging and significance when they are treated with respect. One of the biggest mistakes made by parents and childcare providers is trying to control children instead of teaching them to help and contribute. (More about that later.) Another mistake is to use firmness without kindness (usually punishment) or kindness without firmness (usually permissiveness). Positive Discipline provides the balance.

> Actually, what children (and, for that matter, teenagers and adults) really need is what we call *a sense of belonging and significance.*

All human beings need to belong, to be accepted for who and what they are. Each day of their lives, human beings observe the world around them and the people in it. They have feelings and thoughts about their world, and, most important, they make *decisions* about what it all means. These decisions are rarely conscious, but they are extremely powerful. They form the window through which each of us views our world. Each of us makes decisions as we grow up about whether we are wanted or unwanted, what we must do to survive or thrive, and how we can find love and belonging (or whether we should even try). Our attitudes, choices, and behavior are shaped by the decisions we have made.

> Each of us makes decisions as we grow up about whether we are wanted or unwanted, what we must do to survive or thrive, and how we can find love and belonging.

In this regard, toddlers and preschoolers are no different than adults: They, too, need to belong, and they make daily decisions (usually beyond their conscious awareness) about how to find belonging. Children who know they belong (even when their behavior may not be completely wonderful) feel *en*couraged—and usually behave better. Children who do not believe they belong feel *dis*couraged—and misbehave more often. Wise caregivers will find ways to create a solid sense of belonging and significance for each child in their care. We will explore many ways to accomplish this important goal in the pages ahead.

Get into a Child's World

THINK FOR A moment about the children in your center. What would it be like to see yourself through their eyes? Well, for one thing, you'd have to look

up quite a ways; being smaller than everyone else can create a sense of being "one-down." For another, you would constantly find yourself being asked to do, feel, and think things that were new or unfa-miliar—things like sharing, standing in line, taking turns, coming when called, and so on.

There is *always* a belief behind behavior, even when the person in question doesn't know precisely what that belief might be. One of the best ways to create belonging, shape behavior, and build re-spectful relationships is to get into each child's world, to understand all the complex factors that make him the person he is. We will spend an entire

> There is *always* a be-lief behind behavior, even when the person in question doesn't know precisely what that belief might be.

chapter exploring a child's world and learning about the mysteries of develop-ment, personality, and the effect of a child's environment and parenting. For now, recognize that each child is unique, and there is no substitute for simple curiosity about who he is—and who he is becoming. Getting into a child's world will give you clues that can help you avoid power struggles and hassles during your childcare day.

Let the Message of Caring Get Through

ONE OF THE most intriguing pieces of educational research in recent years has a powerful message for caregivers. The research tells us that a child's moti-vation to learn and cooperate depends to a large degree on how she answers the question "Does the teacher *like* me?" Notice that this perception is very much in the heart of the beholder. The teacher may know that she cares about a child, but if the child doesn't *feel* the caring, the message is lost and that child is less likely to feel belonging—or to do her best in the classroom.

Letting children know you care about them may be more complicated than it appears. After all, parents love their children and rely on that bond of love to get them through the challenges and difficulties of early childhood. (Someone once joked that God made babies cute so parents would keep them despite the mess and fuss they make.) Caregivers and teachers certainly care about children—many care deeply indeed and have chosen their profession out of a deep sense of concern for young children. But does that sense of caring get through to the children?

James Tunney and James Jenkins conducted a research project for their doctoral dissertation on perceptions of caring. They asked teachers whether they cared about their students and were assured that they did. However, when they asked the students whether the teachers cared, they perceived only conditional caring: "The teacher cares only about students who do well."[1]

> Caregivers aren't expected to love each child, but they can choose to treat each child in their care with respect, kindness, and compassion.

If the children in your care could answer the question "Does your teacher or childcare provider care about you?" how do you think they would respond? Adults talk a lot about unconditional caring, but does that message get through to children? Caregivers aren't expected to love each child, but they *can* choose to treat each child in their care with respect, kindness, and compassion. And they can find ways to let even the most challenging little one know that she is cared about, each and every day. Caring and belonging can melt the heart of even the most stubborn preschooler.

The Four Mistaken Goals of Misbehavior

AS WE HAVE learned, children need a sense of belonging and significance. When they do not feel that sense of belonging, they become discouraged. And when children are discouraged, they are likely to misbehave. Dealing with children's misbehavior, especially when those children are in active groups, is one of the greatest challenges caregivers face. Understanding *why* misbehavior happens is an important step toward changing it.

Consider the following scene in a childcare facility much like yours:

Miss Amy, the teacher of the four-year-old class, is watching Tyler and Zachary build a tower of Legos. Just as Tyler prepares to place the flag proudly on the tower, the direc-

---

1.   James Joseph Tunney and James Mancel Jenkins, *A Comparison of Climate as Perceived by Selected Students, Faculty, and Administrators in PASCL, Innovative and Other High Schools.* (Ph.D. dissertation, University of Southern California, 1975.)

DOES THE TEACHER LIKE ME?

Get together with other teachers or childcare providers and brainstorm for a list of specific ways to demonstrate unconditional caring. The list might include such simple things as smiles, handshakes, asking for help, and verbalizing "I care about you." (As we have seen, the list should not include praise or rewards.) Then post your list; make sure you are doing at least one thing from the list every day with every child.

tor walks over to speak to Amy. Tyler waits patiently—for a four-year-old. But as the conversation drags on, Amy and the director are suddenly interrupted by a shrill yelp. Zachary is now sprawling on the carpet, and Tyler is clutching the flag in his fist, a scowl creasing his face.

"Boys," Amy says gently, "please play nicely together while I talk to Mrs. Trent." There is silence for a moment or two, but then Tyler begins to cry. A glance reveals that Zachary now has the flag, and Tyler is crumpled on the carpet. Amy sighs. "Okay, boys," she says, "give me the flag. You can both go to the time-out bench."

When children are discouraged, they are likely to misbehave.

What happened? Well, when the director diverted Amy's attention, the boys' fragile sense of belonging took a blow. They did what most four-year-olds do: They found a way to attract their teacher's attention again. She reprimanded them and they played nicely for a moment, but when she did not return her attention to them, they found another way to demand it. (It is important to recognize that all children need attention and care. However, they do not need to be the "center of attention" all of the time.)

If Amy had been familiar with mistaken goal behavior, she might have recognized her feeling of annoyance as a sign that the children believed they needed "undue attention" to help them feel belonging. She could then have redirected them to find belonging in a useful way by saying, "Boys, I really need your help, and I have faith in you to figure out a solution to this problem. You can tell me about your solution as soon as I'm through talking." Amy could also work with the boys to help them discover ways to entertain themselves and feel content without the constant attention of adults.

The Mistaken Goals of Misbehavior are common ways that children try to create a misguided sense of belonging. They are as follows:

- Undue attention
- Misguided power
- Revenge
- Assumed inadequacy (giving up)

Note that children do not plan out a mistaken goal; they are not even aware of the hidden beliefs behind what they do. But recognizing and understanding the Mistaken Goals can give you options for working with behavior—and for changing the beliefs behind it. (See the Mistaken Goals Chart.)

Undue Attention

You will know a child's mistaken goal is undue attention when you feel irritated, annoyed (as Amy did in the preceding example), worried, or guilty. This is a child who believes she belongs only when she is receiving special service or keeping an adult busy with her—not an uncommon situation in this age of pampered, overindulged children. Undue attention is a common goal, especially for young children, who often equate attention with love and caring. The last column of the Mistaken Goals Chart will give you tools to use to address the mistaken goal of undue attention. (We will explain those tools in detail in the pages ahead.)

Misguided Power

This mistaken goal is also especially popular among preschoolers, who are developmentally inclined to exercise their growing sense of autonomy and personal power. Adults seem to create power struggles with children when they

don't recognize this important stage of child development. You will know this is a child's mistaken goal when you feel provoked, challenged, threatened, or defeated. The goal of misguided power gives you opportunities to practice giving choices, asking for help, being firm and kind, and allowing children (three and older) to choose positive time-out if they think that will help (page 40). Again, the last column of the Mistaken Goals Chart will give you tools and options for dealing with this mistaken goal.

Revenge

When children resort to the mistaken goal of revenge, their behavior can be downright ugly and hurtful. This behavior can be especially troubling in the preschool, as it can cause deep feelings for both children and adults. You will know a child is seeking revenge when you feel hurt, disappointed, disbelieving, or disgusted—even when you are not the target of the child's hurtful behavior. In a preschool setting, revenge can happen because a child feels unfairly dealt with (another drawback of relying on excessive control to manage behavior) or because of something happening at home, such as parents who are divorcing or the loss of a pet or loved one. Punishment never helps a child who is seeking revenge; instead, rely on active listening, understand and validate the child's

> You will know a child is seeking revenge when you feel hurt, disappointed, disbelieving, or disgusted—even when you are not the target of the child's hurtful behavior.

Mistaken Goals Chart

The Child's Goal Is:	If the Parent/ Teacher Feels:	And Tends to React by:	And if the Child's Response Is:
Undue attention (to keep others busy or to get special service)	Annoyed; irritated; worried; guilty	Reminding; coaxing; doing things for the child he could do for himself	Stops temporarily, but later resumes same or another disturbing behavior
Misguided power (to be boss)	Provoked; challenged; threatened; defeated	Fighting; giving in; thinking: "You can't get away with it" or "I'll make you"; wanting to be right	Intensifies behavior; defiant compliance; feels he's won when parent/ teacher is upset; passive power
Revenge (to get even)	Hurt, disappointed; disbelieving; disgusted	Retaliating; getting even; thinking, "How could you do this to me?"	Retaliates; intensifies; escalates the same behavior or chooses another weapon
Assumed inadequacy (to give up and be left alone)	Despair; hopeless; helpless; inadequate	Giving up; doing for; overhelping	Retreats further; passive; no improvement no response

THE BELIEF BEHIND THE CHILD'S BEHAVIOR IS:	CHILD'S MESSAGES:	PARENT/TEACHER PROACTIVE AND EMPOWERING RESPONSES INCLUDE:
I count (belong) only when I'm being noticed or getting special service; I'm only important when I'm keeping you busy with me	"Notice me, involve me"	"I love you and _____." (Example: I care about you and will spend time with you later.); redirect by assigning a task so child can gain useful attention; avoid special ; service plan special time; set up routines; use problem-solving; encourage; use family/class metings; touch without words; ignore; set up nonverbal signals
I belong only when I'm boss, in control, or proving no one can boss me; "You can't make me"	"Let me help; give me choices"	Redirect to positive power by asking for help; offer limited choices; don't fight and don't give in; withdraw from conflict; be firm and kind; act, don't talk; decide what you will do; let routines be the boss; leave and calm down; develop mutual respect; set a few reasonable limits; practice follow-through; encourage; use family/class meetings
I don't think I belong, so I'll hurt others as I feel hurt; I can't be liked or loved	"Help me, I'm hurting; acknowledge my feelings"	Acknowledge the hurt feelings; avoid feeling hurt; avoid punishment and retaliation; build trust; use reflective listening; share your feelings; make amends; show that you care; act, don't talk; encourage strengths; put kids in same boat; use family/class meetings
I can't belong because I'm not perfect, so I'll convince others not to expect anything of me; I am helpless and unable; it's no use trying because I won't do it right	"Show me small steps; celebrate my successes"	Break task down to small steps; stop all criticism; encourage any positive attempt; have faith in child's ability; focus on assets; don't give up; set up opportunities for success; teach skills/show how, but don't do for; enjoy the child; build on his interests; encourage, encourage, encourage; use family/class meetings

feelings, and share your own feelings. After this has been done (and only after) you can help the child discover ways to make amends.

Assumed Inadequacy

This is the child who "can't," even though developmentally he could. He can't ride the tricycle, button his own sweater, or do a puzzle. He often won't meet your eyes, hangs his head, and looks so discouraged you want to cry yourself. Adults often step in to "help" the child who is giving up—or they give up on the child themselves. You will know this is a child's mistaken goal when you feel despairing, helpless, hopeless, or inadequate yourself. This behavior needs lots of caring encouragement to heal. Hard as it can be, focus on small steps, offer encouragement, and don't step in to rescue.

> Understanding the belief behind a child's behavior is one of the most effective ways to encourage children and to bring out their best.

It is important to recognize that one behavior can be caused by any of the four goals. A child may refuse to pick up the blocks in the play area because he wants your attention (you feel irritated and annoyed), to show you you're "not the boss of him" (you feel provoked and challenged), to hurt you as he's been hurt (you feel hurt yourself), or because he is deeply discouraged and wants to be left alone (you feel hopeless and helpless). Understanding the belief behind a child's behavior is one of the most effective ways to encourage children and to bring out their best.

It is important to remember also that any of these behaviors can be a developmental issue instead of a *misbehavior*—especially for children aged three and under. Many a two-year-old will engage you in a power struggle, not because he feels discouraged or feels belonging only if he is in charge. He is simply following his age-appropriate clock to develop his sense of autonomy and his desires to explore and experiment, and feels very frustrated when thwarted in his efforts. More about this in chapter 4.

Discipline That Is Kind and Firm

IN THE BOOK *Parents Who Love Too Much*,[2] we explored the risks of extremes in parenting, the consequences of being either excessively controlling or permissive. Excessive control and permissiveness don't happen only in children's homes, however; extremes happen every day in childcare centers as well.

Many childcare providers rely on control, including punishment and rewards, to manage children's behavior. There are lots of rules and lots of "consequences" for breaking them. One frustrated parent tells the story of her three-year-old son Robby's former childcare center, at which the children were expected to "line up" for bathroom time and to sit at tables to play with their toys. Not surprisingly, many of the children in this center, including Robby, became "discipline problems." Excessive control usually encourages rebellion, defiance, power struggles, or sneakiness—not the results most caregivers want to produce. Robby's misbehavior ceased when he moved to a new childcare center, one with rules and expectations more in line with his developmental abilities.

> Neither excessive control nor permissiveness creates respectful, responsible, capable children.

You might not think caregivers would be prone to permissiveness; overindulgence, rescuing, and unwillingness to follow through with consequences or

---

2. Authored by Jane Nelsen and Cheryl Erwin (Roseville, CA: Prima, 2000).

agreements seem to be problems parents would have, not teachers or childcare staff. Yet in the busy, sometimes noisy environment of a childcare facility, it can be hard to stay focused, to do what you have said, or to take the time to practice consistent, effective discipline. Unfortunately, neither excessive control nor permissiveness creates respectful, responsible, capable children.

> Being kind and firm at the same time means you do not need to yell; it means children can rely on the fact that you mean what you say and say what you mean.

The solution, we believe, is learning to be *kind and firm at the same time*—kind because you respect the inherent worth and dignity of each child, and firm because you respect yourself and the needs of the situation. Children need boundaries and structure; consistent, respectful discipline is one of the ways they learn trust and feel secure. Being kind and firm at the same time means you do not need to yell; it means children can rely on the fact that you mean what you say and say what you mean, and that you can follow through with dignity and respect. (For example, you can kindly take a child by the hand and firmly show him what he can do instead of yelling at him for what he can't do.) It also means that your center becomes a place where discipline is a pleasure to watch and to do, and where no child (and no teacher) needs to suffer humiliation, shame, or discouragement.

Positive Discipline Tools

WE EXAMINED THE myths and misconceptions behind most approaches to "discipline" in chapter 2. Here we'll take a closer look at specific Positive Discipline tools you can use to implement respectful discipline in your childcare center. What does kind, firm discipline really look like?

Decide What *You* Will Do

It is tempting to decide what children (or coworkers, or spouses, or friends) should do. Indeed, many of us try to do just that: We wheedle, manipulate, lecture, bribe, or punish. But the truth is that the only person you can truly control is yourself—and even that is a challenge sometimes! (Well, you can control a young child for a while just because you are bigger; but you may pay a high price in future misbehavior as a result.) Part of kind, firm discipline is deciding what *you* will do, then following through with dignity and respect.

Katie was tired of nagging, reminding, and coaxing her three-year-olds to gather up their mats after quiet time so she could begin reading a story. She raised her voice; the children chattered louder and asked her continually when she would begin reading.

One day Katie decided that she would not nag anymore. Just before quiet time, when the children were quiet and settled on their mats, she told them kindly but firmly that after quiet time, she would begin reading the story when they had picked up their mats and were sitting quietly in a circle.

> Part of kind, firm discipline is deciding what you will do, then following through with dignity and respect.

When quiet time ended, the children began their usual buzz of noise and activity. But this time something was different. Instead of coaxing and reminding the children, Katie sat quietly in her chair with a favorite book in her lap. When the children clamored for her to read, she simply smiled and pointed to the mats on the floor. It didn't take long for one or two of the children to figure out what was happening. "Hurry up," they called to the other children, "let's pick up our mats so Miss Katie can read to us."

As Katie discovered, controlling your own behavior is almost always more effective than trying to control the behavior of others.

Act, Don't Talk

Adults like to use words. We're good at talking, so we do a lot of it. Children, however, don't always respond well to talking, especially when it comes in the form of nagging or lecturing. Remember those old *Peanuts* videos? Remember how the adults always sounded? (*Blah, blah, blaahhh* . . .). And how often have you found yourself in a heated debate with someone who comes up to your kneecap—and lost?

Children often ignore words when those words are not accompanied by action. Words can also become fuel for a power struggle. ("Pick up the toys." "No!") Try using kind, firm action instead of words the next time you want cooperation from a young child. Take the hand of the little boy who refuses to leave the play area and gently guide him over for circle time. Remove a toy from children who are struggling over it and, with a kind smile, place it out of reach; they will understand without words that they can have the toy back when they stop fighting over it.

> Children often ignore words when those words are not accompanied by action.

Also, when you must talk, be sure you don't issue commands or instructions from across the room; children know they can safely ignore a talking adult who isn't within arm's reach. Stand up and walk toward children while speaking in a kind, firm voice; action will make it clear that you mean what you say.

Use Very Few Words

Have you ever noticed how adults often talk on and on and on—lecturing as though children were hanging on every word. If they were paying closer attention to the children, they would see that they are hardly listening at all.

Obviously there are times when you have to say something. When acting without talking isn't enough, use very few words, and eliminate the "don'ts." Include the "dos."

Eighteen-month-old Sage started hitting other children in her daycare provider's home. Maria, her daycare provider, started watching very closely. When she noticed Sage starting to hit, she quickly (but kindly) caught her arm and said, "Touch nicely." Maria then guided Sage's hand to gently stroke the other child's arm. Sage seemed to enjoy "touching nicely," but later would start to hit again. After Maria had guided her in gentle touching for about a week, she would notice Sage starting to hit and would say, "Touch nicely" without guiding her hand. Sage would grin and touch nicely.

The hitting didn't totally disappear for about a month, but Maria enjoyed this kind of discipline much more than her former yelling and/or long explanations about why a child shouldn't hit. "And," she smiled, "the yelling and lectures didn't work any faster."

Follow Through

Most adults agree that the biggest hurdle they must overcome in providing effective discipline is actually *doing* what they say. Sometimes this is because adults make threats or concoct consequences when they are frustrated or angry, and they know that acting on rash words will only make the situation worse. Sometimes adults don't follow through because they are unwilling to endure children's crying or whining, or they don't want children to be "unhappy."

Effective discipline, which creates cooperative, secure children, requires that adults follow through. That means teachers and caregivers must give careful thought to what they say and be willing to act without nagging, lecturing, or shaming. As Dreikurs has said, "Shut your mouth and act."

Five-year-old Nikki came to preschool one bright fall morning with some interesting new words—the four-letter variety. When Nikki tried her new vocabulary on her teacher, Barbara overreacted.

"Nikki!" Barbara said firmly, "Don't you ever let me hear you use that word in this school again!"

Not surprisingly, Nikki was delighted with the result of her experiment; it was fun to create such excitement! The next day, she tried another of her new words, but this time Barbara was prepared.

She said, "I'm going to go over to the dress-up corner now to see what the other children are doing. Let me know when you're ready to speak respectfully."

Nikki didn't find her new words nearly as entertaining without an audience. Later that day, Barbara found time for a quiet talk with Nikki. "Most people don't like hearing the words you used earlier," she told Nikki. "If you choose to use them in the future, you can go to the cool-off spot until you can feel better and others can't hear you, or I will go to another part of the room for a while. It's up to you."

Now all Barbara has to do is follow through. Her plan worked so well, in fact, that several days later she heard one of Nikki's friends saying a bad word. Nikki responded, "That isn't respectful. I'm going to play with someone else until you're ready to stop using those words."

Here are some ways to tell whether your follow-through will be effective in teaching children:

- Is the response respectful to the child, the teacher, and the needs of the situation?

- Does it allow for differences in temperament?
- Is it encouraging children to gain confidence and self-reliance?
- Does it teach life skills for now and for the future?

Remember, the way you interact with children will be teaching them about mutual respect, dignity, and responsibility—gifts that will benefit them for the rest of their lives.

Offer Choices—Wisely

You may have noticed in the prior example that Barbara offered Nikki choices about ways to deal with her profanity. Choices can be a marvelous tool for your teaching toolbox, but it is important to think carefully about the choices you offer a child—and to be sure that *each* choice is acceptable to you.

Four-year-old Rodney loved to climb to the top of the jungle gym in his childcare provider's back yard. One afternoon during playtime, he refused to come down when Linda clapped her hands for the children to return indoors. Linda stood looking up at Rodney and, with no small amount of frustration, said, "Do you want to climb down, or do I have to come up and get you?" This possibility was just too appealing for Rodney to turn down; he grinned slyly and stayed perched firmly atop the jungle gym. Linda gamely climbed up to get him, but she learned to think through her choices before offering them!

Offer choices that are reasonable, acceptable to you, and respectful of both the child and the situation, and then follow through with dignity and respect.

One method of offering children choices (particularly young children who may need help in weighing alternatives) is to prepare a "Wheel of Choice" during a class meeting. Invite your group to brainstorm some suggestions for common classroom problems (more on class meetings in a moment). Then put each suggestion in one "slice" of the circle, with a spinner in the center. For instance, choices might include "Use your words," "Take a positive time-out," "Ask for help," "Help the other person," "Choose another toy," and so on. When difficulties arise in your class, the child with the problem can be invited to choose one of the suggestions or spin the wheel to decide what to try.

Remember, offer choices that are reasonable, acceptable to you, and respectful of both the child and the situation, and then follow through with dignity and respect. It is especially empowering to a child when you say, "You decide," after giving a choice.

Focus on Solutions

Most folks who work with children these days have heard of consequences. We have found, however, that *consequences* often is just another word for *punishment*. Nonpunitive consequences, both natural and logical, can be a valuable teaching tool and an effective part of childcare discipline. But it is usually better to focus on finding a *solution* to a problem, rather than searching for "the" consequence that will resolve it.

Many different Positive Discipline tools can be solutions, and it is important to realize that no one tool, no matter how useful, will work in all situations with all children. Understanding the beliefs behind behavior, getting into a child's world, and focusing on solutions will almost always lead to improvement in a difficult situation. Still, most caregivers have questions about consequences. What are they, and when is it a good idea to use them?

> No one tool, no matter how useful, will work in all situations with all children.

Take Advantage of Natural Consequences

Natural consequences are those things that happen as a result of our own choices. If you go outside in the rain and refuse to wear your raincoat, you will get very wet. If you refuse to eat a meal, you will get hungry. If you don't go to bed at a reasonable hour, you will be tired the next morning. Children can learn from natural consequences when adults get out of the way and don't lecture or nag. For instance, you might say, "Goodness, your clothes are wet! Can you think of a way to dry off and feel better?"

Use Logical Consequences

When there is no natural consequence for a behavior (or the natural consequence is unacceptable, such as the result of playing in the middle of the street), adults may substitute a logical consequence. When you tear the clothes in the dress-up corner, you can help repair them. When you take snack food to the play area, you may have to spend your time cleaning up the crumbs instead of playing.

Attitude is everything when using consequences. If you set up a consequence with a desire to shame or humiliate a child, it will feel like a punishment (actually, it will *be* a punishment), and the child will respond accordingly. To be effective, consequences must be directly related to the misbehavior, reasonable, and respectful. As with all discipline, a kind but firm approach is essential.

Attitude is everything when using consequences.

The point of consequences is to help children learn for the future. Punishment is designed to make children "pay" for what they did instead of learn from it. (We know some people think children learn from punishment—and they do. They learn resentment, rebellion, not to get caught, or that they are "bad." They also learn to punish others.)

An effective way to use logical consequences is to help the child explore the consequences of his choices through "what" and "how" questions (discussed later in this chapter). This is much different from imposing a consequence on the child. For example, when a child tears clothing in the dress-up corner you could ask, "What happened? What do you think caused that to happen? What ideas do you have to solve the problem?" Children four years of age and older

usually have very creative ideas for solutions. And this process helps them learn thinking skills, problem-solving skills, consequences of their choices, concern for others—and a sense of belonging and significance.

Remember the discussion on changing your vocabulary to change your behavior? You might ask yourself, "What is a good solution for this problem? What will help prevent the problem in the future?" Taking time to think this through will give you much more positive results than asking, "What is the consequence for this behavior?"

Use Positive Time-Out

> It is simple but true: Children *do* better when they *feel* better.

Even though the National Association for the Education of Young Children (NAEYC) strongly opposes time-out, many preschools and childcare centers still use some form of time-out. Time-out usually consists of sending a child off to sit or stand alone and "think about what he did." Aside from the fact that you cannot control what a child thinks about (and he is more likely to be thinking about how mad he is at you than what he contributed to the situation), time-out is rarely effective in the *long term* when used in a punitive way.

It is simple but true. Children *do* better when they *feel* better. Like adults, sometimes emotions overwhelm children, and they just can't quite settle down to work on solutions, change their behavior, or behave the way they should. Time-out, when used in a positive way, can give children a moment to "cool off," to feel better so that they can participate in problem solving and change their behavior.

Consider creating (or, better yet, having the children help you create) a time-out spot in your center. One teacher filled an old, claw-footed bathtub with pillows and stuffed animals; another opened up an old refrigerator box to create a cozy "cave" and filled it with blankets, koosh balls, books, and other soothing objects. Another created a nook decorated like outer space for when children needed "space." Because time-out usually implies punishment, ask the children to give it another name such as "our happy place," "the feel-good place," or "space." When a child is misbehaving, is angry, or just can't get along with others, you may ask her whether the time-out spot would help her "feel better." (If children aren't old enough to help create it and to choose it, they are not old enough for this to be an effective tool.)

> When the child has had time to cool off *and is ready to change her behavior,* she can rejoin the others.

If a child does go to the cool-off spot, you can even go with her, if you choose, or let her choose another child to go with her. When she has had time to cool off *and is ready to change her behavior,* she can rejoin the others. Remember, children want to belong, so they will not want to stay in even a pleasant time-out forever. You may be surprised to discover that children will put themselves in positive time-out, when the time-out helps them to feel and do better. When they feel better, if it is appropriate, you can help them find a solution to the problem. Children aren't very receptive to problem solving when they are upset. Come to think of it, neither are adults.

Some caregivers worry that they are rewarding children for poor behavior by allowing them to do "fun" things in time-out. Positive time-out is a way to teach children the important life skill of taking time to calm down to feel better and then do better—a skill that will serve them all their lives.[3] It is important to remember that even positive time-out should never be the only discipline option. You might try asking a child, "What would help you the most right now—the Wheel of Choice or our feel-good place?" This approach helps children learn self-discipline and self-control.

---

3. For more information on positive time-out, see Jane Nelsen, *Positive Time-Out and 50 Ways to Avoid Power Struggles* (Roseville, CA: Prima, 2000).

Establish Routines

Young children love predictability and consistency; in fact, routines help them learn and feel comfortable in their world. Wise caregivers understand this, and they build routines into each facet of the childcare day. Clear expectations and predictable activities can smooth the rough spots out of a youngster's day (and that of his teachers and parents, as well).

Young children love predictability and consistency; in fact, routines help them learn and feel comfortable in their world.

You probably cannot have too many routines in your childcare facility. Children should know what to expect when they arrive, during transition times, at snack time, at quiet time, at circle time, and when they leave. They also should know which activity follows which. You may find routines boring and enjoy the day more when you vary your activities, but you are likely to see much better behavior from the children and have a much smoother day yourself when you do things the same way at the same time each and every day.

One way of organizing routines for children is to make routine charts. Get some large pieces of poster board, bright markers, glitter, and perhaps photographs or pictures cut from magazines of children performing various activities (or take digital or Polaroid photographs of the children actually doing the tasks). List the day's tasks in order, illustrating each one with a picture. You may want to make separate charts for more complex activities, such as circle

Once a routine has become familiar, the routine becomes the "boss."

time or mealtimes. Then post your charts where they are at a child's eye level. Once a routine has become familiar, the routine becomes the "boss." When children get off-task or are distracted by something, you can simply ask them, "What is next in our routine?" Older children can help you create routines and can help make charts themselves. (Remember, when children have a voice in setting up the rules, they are more likely to follow them!)

Hold Class Meetings

It is class meeting time at the ABC Preschool. As the youngsters settle into a circle, Mr. Scott, the teacher, consults the agenda.

"It sounds like we've had a problem on the playground with people throwing wood chips at one another. Does anyone have something to say about this problem, or can someone offer a suggestion of how we might solve it?"

Five-year-old Girard raises his hand. "Whoever throws wood chips could take a time-out!" Four-year-old Natalie waves her hand, and when called upon, offers, "We could not have wood chips anymore and have grass instead."

The teacher looks toward three-year-old Christina, whose little hand has been patiently held aloft, and calls on her. "Guess what?" Christina says with a bright smile.

"What, Christina?" Mr. Scott asks.

"I had bananas in my cereal today."

"Mmmm, that must have tasted good." Mr. Scott smiles and thanks Christina for her comment, then asks for more suggestions about the wood chip problem. Although Christina clearly was not thinking about wood chips, she was still a valued member of the group. When children are old enough to participate actively in group or circle time activities (usually around the age of three), they are ready for class meetings.[4]

Class meetings provide a priceless opportunity for children to learn respect, problem solving, social skills, language development, and encouragement. And you might be surprised at how effective class meetings can be in

---

4. From Jane Nelsen, Cheryl Erwin, and Roslyn Duffy, *Positive Discipline for Preschoolers*, rev. 2d ed.(Roseville, CA: Prima, 1998), p. 203.

resolving the problems that arise for all caregivers and the children they work with. If you have children of different ages in your center, the older ones can serve as role models and mentors for the little ones. If you have only three- or four-year-olds in your group, you can coach them in learning the skills of working together and model those skills for them.

Class meetings provide a priceless opportunity for children to learn respect, problem solving, social skills, language development, and encouragement.

The sidebar shows the four elements of class meetings for preschoolers. Let's take a closer look at each in the next sections.

Giving Compliments and Appreciation

Why is it important to teach children to give and receive compliments and appreciation? Like adults, children need to learn to see and appreciate the positive—to become "good finders"—and they need opportunities to practice having an attitude of gratitude. Also, beginning your class meetings with compliments starts things off on a positive, friendly note and invites everyone in the group to contribute and feel valued.

Children often lack experience in noticing what's right in their world; like parents and teachers, they're sometimes better at noticing what's wrong. Caregivers can ask some helpful questions to get the process started. "What is something you like about our school?" or "Is there someone who helped you feel good today?" can teach children to offer meaningful compliments to each other. Activities like "Kid of the Week" may also be encouraging ways to

FOUR ELEMENTS OF CLASS MEETINGS FOR PRESCHOOLERS

- To give compliments and appreciation
- To empower children to help each other
- To solve problems that affect the group
- To plan future activities

> Like adults, children need to learn to see and appreciate the positive—to become "good finders."

begin your class meeting. (Be careful not to make these activities into rewards for achievement or good behavior.)

Empowering Children to Help Each Other

Imagine what the world might be like if each of us could ask for help when we need it and offer help to those around us. You have the opportunity to teach this valuable ability to the children in your center by giving them time during each class meeting to ask for help from the group. The following story from *Positive Discipline for Preschoolers* gives you an example:

> It is Tuesday morning at the Hill Harbor Child Care Center. The class of three- and four-year-olds is just beginning their class meeting with their teacher, Mr. Silk. He asks if anyone needs help from the group today.
>
> Matthias raises his hand and announces, "I can't wake up in the morning." Many of the other children agree that it's hard for them, too. Mr. Silk asks if anyone has a suggestion for Matthias. The children offer all sorts of helpful ideas: "Go to bed earlier." "Get up anyway." "Come to school in pajamas."
>
> Mr. Silk turns to Matthias. "Do you think any of these ideas will help you, or should the group think of some more?" Matthias pauses to consider, then says he is going to "get up anyway."
>
> Next, Julian raises his hand and says he needs help because "My mom doesn't have enough money." After sympathizing with Julian, other children volunteer that they have that problem, too. Julian's friends are eager to help. Some of the children offer to bring in money. Bobby suggests that Julian could do some jobs to get money. Katie says, "My mom will help." Devon recommends, "Your mom can get a job that makes more money."
>
> It is unlikely that Julian's mom will have more money as a result of this discussion. But Julian has learned that his friends will listen respectfully to him and will try to help when they can. He has also learned that his classmates care about him and sometimes face similar worries. "Helping each other" can become a powerful part of class meetings.

Solving Problems

Even young children can be remarkably creative when it comes to solving problems—and they certainly love to be asked! Consider posting an "agenda board" in a convenient spot in your center. Whenever a problem or concern arises, you can invite children to write their problem on the agenda to be discussed at the next class meeting. (Children too young to write may need help from you, or can draw a letter or picture on the agenda.) Then, during problem-solving time, each agenda item can be addressed in turn.

It is both fun and productive to brainstorm with children. Ask for solutions to the problem at hand and write down each one. (Older children can take turns being the recorder or running the meeting.) Don't dismiss or allow ridicule of any idea; the point of brainstorming is that even a silly or unworkable suggestion may lead to a good one. When brainstorming is complete, you can help the child with the problem choose a solution. (It is often helpful to use "what" and "how" questions to make sure the solution chosen is respectful to everyone concerned.) Using a "talking stick" or passing around a stuffed animal for the speaker to hold can help keep the process from getting too noisy or enthusiastic.

> Don't dismiss or allow ridicule of any idea; the point of brainstorming is that even a silly or unworkable suggestion may lead to a good one.

Imagine what might happen if, instead of scolding children for breaking a toy and forbidding them to use the play area for the rest of the day, you put "broken toys" on the class meeting agenda and invited the children to find solutions to the problem. The children now have the opportunity to learn good judgment, creativity, social skills, and mutual respect—a result that might even be worth a broken toy!

Planning Future Activities

Involving children in planning an activity almost always makes that activity more successful. You can invite children's help in planning future field trips, class activities, treats, or fund-raisers. Again, hearing suggestions respectfully and diplomatically keeping suggestions reasonable ("Let's all go to Disneyland!" probably isn't going to happen) will make this an enjoyable and useful part of your class meeting.

Suggestions for Success

Here are some tips for making the most of class meetings:

- Be aware of timing. Depending on the age, development, and abilities of the children in your group, you may need to keep meetings short or do only one thing per meeting. It is better to have shorter meetings every day than to have a meeting only once a week. Children need to practice class meetings on a daily basis to master the skills. No matter how you decide to use them, class meetings can still be an effective part of your childcare routine.

> Involving children in planning an activity almost always makes that activity more successful.

- Special signals may help children stay in step with you. For instance, you may use a special song or gesture to signal the beginning and end of a meeting, to ask for quiet, or to move on to a new topic. Children often respond better to actions and signals than they do to words.

- You can vote when appropriate if it concerns a group activity. However, it is not appropriate to allow the group to vote on a solution for another person. Use wisdom: Voting can create winners and losers—and losers often lose interest in the process. Aim for decisions by consensus whenever possible.

- Keep notes of each meeting so you remember what was decided, what was tabled, and what needs to be addressed the next time the group gets together.

- You may be surprised at how little "classroom management" is necessary when you teach children the skills for effective class meetings.

Offer Special Time

Miss Marsha is everyone's favorite childcare provider. The neighborhood children all love being at her house, and parents tell each other, "Oh, you're so lucky—your child is at Marsha's!" Marsha's secret of success is that she practices encouraging the children she cares for each day, noticing their small efforts and triumphs. One thing she has discovered works very well is to find a few moments for "special time" with each child, one-on-one time during the day when she can focus her attention on one child.

She may greet three-year-old Richard with a question about his favorite television show; she asks six-year-old Caitlin whether her mom read her the next chapter in Harry Potter last night. Marsha knows something special about each of the children in her care and always takes time to let them know she's thinking of them. Although life isn't perfect, Marsha's kids behave beautifully (most of the time) and are eager to volunteer when she asks for their help. They feel noticed and special; they know she likes them.

"Special time" is a wonderful way of connecting with each child and allowing him or her to feel the energy of your caring. You need not spend a great deal of time; just a few moments each day is probably enough to send the message that you are interested. You may greet each child as he arrives in the morning, have a quiet word with him just before quiet time, or send him home with a personal compliment. Whatever you do, finding some special time with each child can make an astonishing difference in the atmosphere in your center.

> "Special time" is a wonderful way of connecting with each child and allowing him or her to feel the energy of your caring.

Communicating with Children

MANY CAREGIVERS TAKE communication with children for granted; adults talk, children listen (or they're supposed to). But communicating with young children, especially children who are just developing their language skills, is an art. The more effective you are, the better your day (and that of the children) is likely to go.

Children do not perceive the world as adults do, nor do even the most articulate of them have words for everything they sense, feel, and want. Take a moment sometime and watch a toddler or preschooler try to deal with frustration or anger. She may throw a toy across the room, stamp her foot, fall over backward in a tantrum, or collapse in a flood of tears. She may do all of these at practically the same instant. And lecturing, scolding, or issuing instructions is unlikely to help her sort out what has happened, how she feels, and what she should do next. Keeping a few concepts in mind will help you understand and help the children you care for.

The Role of Nonverbal Communication

Children are keen observers of nonverbal communication. Because they do not have language when they are born, they learn about the world around them by observing. They watch facial expressions; they hear tone of voice. They notice body position and the energy of feelings. As they grow, they become aware that adults' words sometimes do not match their nonverbal messages. In fact, communications theory teaches that as much as 80 percent of the message we communicate to others lies in our nonverbal signals rather than our words. Young children instinctively trust your face, your body, and the energy of your feelings more than your words alone.

> Communications theory teaches that as much as 80 percent of the message we communicate to others lies in our nonverbal signals rather than our words.

It was music time at the Elm Street Preschool. The children all loved playing with the instruments and making music together, but their teacher, Janice, had a headache, and the mere thought of the cymbals crashing, the drums smashing, and the flutes shrilling made her temples throb.

"Okay, kids, let's go to the music table," she said with as much enthusiasm as she could muster. As the children chose instruments and began to toot them experimentally, four-year-old Andrew tugged at Janice's skirt.

"Don't you like our song, Miss Janice?" he asked.

"Of course, I do," Janice answered.

"Then why is your forehead all scrunched up?" Andrew replied.

Children often know what adults are thinking and feeling before adults do. When working with young children, it is helpful to be sure that your words and your nonverbal messages match up. Get down on a child's level so that you can look him in the eyes when you speak to him, smile, and use a warm tone of voice. Children will feel much more comfortable in your presence when you can attend to the nonverbal impact of your communication—and theirs.

Practice Active Listening

Children have lots of feelings. In fact, they can experience an entire spectrum of emotions within a few minutes. But some adults are astonished to learn that children often don't have *words* to go with their feelings. And when a child doesn't quite understand what is happening (or when he doesn't feel understood), he probably won't be able to listen to suggestions or work on his behavior effectively.

> Some adults are astonished to learn that children often don't have *words* to go with their feelings.

One of the best ways to help children communicate is to practice *active* (or *reflective*) *listening*. This means noticing what a child is feeling (it's okay to guess and to rely on the child's nonverbal language) and simply sharing what you notice. It does not mean that you agree with a child's feelings; but in noticing and commenting, you will let the child know you care and build a foundation for later problem solving.

> As the children enjoyed music time, Janice noticed that one little girl sat alone without an instrument.
>
> "Karen, you look pretty sad," Janice said kindly.
>
> Karen looked up into her teacher's face, and her lower lip began to tremble. "Sarah took my horn," she said. "And now there aren't any more things to blow."
>
> Janice reached out a hand. "Let's go see what we can find for you to play," she offered, as Karen took her hand and stood up. "Maybe Sarah will be willing to share the horn with you later."

Notice that Janice didn't rescue Karen, nor did she offer solutions until she'd reflected Karen's feelings. Karen might have corrected her teacher, saying, "I'm not sad—I'm mad at Sarah." Either way, active listening allows children to label and understand their emotions, to feel understood, and to move on to dealing with the issue at hand.

Ask "What" and "How" Questions

It is usually more expedient for adults to *tell* children what to do, when to do it, and how to do it. But one way of encouraging good judgment, as well as building a respectful and caring relationship, is by using "what" and "how" questions in speaking with children. Instead of telling, you can *ask* children (while still giving them hints to solve the problem), encouraging them to think and to take ownership of their own ideas.

> *As Mark gazed at the play area, he noticed three-year-old Marcus working out a complicated logistical problem. Marcus was trying to pick up blocks, but each time he bent over to pick up another block, three or four of those already in his arms fell to the floor. Marcus was becoming more and more frustrated and looked as if he was ready to toss the entire pile to the ground—or at one of the other children.*
>
> *"Hey, bud," Mark said, wandering casually over to Marcus. "Looks like you're getting a little frustrated by those blocks. What would happen if you carried two or three at a time to the shelves?"*
>
> *Marcus paused, scowling. "It would take me longer to pick them up," he said. Then his face brightened. "But I probably wouldn't drop them."*
>
> *Mark smiled. "Do you want to carry them, or do you want my help?" he asked.*
>
> *Marcus stood up straight, three blue blocks balanced carefully in his arms. "I can do it," he said proudly. "Watch me!"*

By using active listening, a "what" question, and choices, Mark allowed Marcus to take ownership of his own problem and find a solution. Advice or unwanted help might have tipped the frustrated three-year-old into a full-fledged tantrum; using good communication skills not only avoided an emotional outburst but ensured that Marcus would experience success at his task—which Mark can then celebrate with him by offering encouragement for his accomplishment.

There are many ways to use "what" and "how" questions to encourage independent thinking, problem solving, and good judgment in young children and to build a mutually respectful relationship with them. Here are some suggestions:

- What made that happen? What would you like to have happen? How could you make that happen next time?
- What things do you like about _____?
- How do you feel when you're playing with _____ (insert name of least desirable playmate)?
- How can I help you?
- What ideas do you have for solving this problem?

Mistakes Are Wonderful Opportunities to Learn

> Learn to see mistakes as gifts, everyday opportunities to learn new ideas, approaches, and skills.

LAST BUT CERTAINLY not least, remember that mistakes—both your own and the children's—can become chances for all of you to learn together. Rather than seeing mistakes as failures or flaws to be ashamed of, learn to see mistakes as gifts, everyday opportunities to learn new ideas, approaches, and skills.

You will undoubtedly make mistakes as you try to implement the ideas in this book—new skills and attitudes always take time to learn. The children you work with will make mistakes, too. You can decide together that you will clean up your messes, apologize when necessary, and then work together to learn how to avoid the mistake next time around. You may discover that your

POSITIVE DISCIPLINE TOOLS FOR CAREGIVERS

- Decide what you will do.
- Act, don't talk.
- Use very few words.
- Follow through.
- Offer choices.
- Focus on solutions.
- Use consequences, both natural and logical, to teach.
- Use positive time-out.
- Establish routines.
- Hold class meetings.
- Offer special time.
- Practice active listening.
- Ask "what" and "how" questions.

childcare facility gets better and better with each mistake, when you and the children can forgive and encourage each other, and remain open to learning new ways of doing things.

These Positive Discipline ideas and tools will help you work with children—and they're surprisingly effective with other adults, too. As we continue through this book, refer back to this chapter. You will find in the chapters ahead more detailed information on how to use Positive Discipline, as well as more in-depth material on getting into the world of the children you see each day and facing the interesting new challenges they present you.

4

A Young Child's World

Understanding Development, Brain Growth, and Temperament

Marcy loves children. She began an in-home childcare business three years ago as a way to earn money and stay home with her own children. Marcy takes her responsibilities seriously. She has satisfied local licensing procedures and goes regularly for extra training. She reads books on discipline and communication and never misses a meeting of her local childcare providers' association. Yet there are days when Marcy wonders what on Earth made her think that running a childcare center was such a great idea. When the last child has been picked up and the last parent has driven away, Marcy often collapses in the nearest chair, utterly exhausted.

In addition to her own two boys, Marcy cares for six children each day from eight in the morning until six at night. All eight children are under the age of six, and the action never stops. Some days, everything goes smoothly and Marcy enjoys her young companions. Other days aren't so wonderful. "They don't listen to me," Marcy tells her husband in frustration one evening. "There are days when they just won't share or get along. They won't do what I ask them to do: If I tell them to go outdoors, they want to stay inside. If I want them to stay inside, they all run outdoors. They won't take a nap. They squabble with each other and throw toys. They don't want to clean up. And they get into absolutely everything. I just don't understand them!"

Most adults have joked at one time or another that part of the problem with young children is that they don't come with an instruction manual. Teachers, caregivers, and parents alike—even the most loving and committed of them—can feel baffled by a preschooler's behavior, by the way she perceives and reacts to her world, and by the way she thinks and feels. Managing one active preschooler can be a challenge; imagine, then, how it feels to spend your days in a room with fifteen or twenty of them. (Then again, perhaps you already know all too well how that feels!) It isn't surprising that most teachers and caregivers tell us that they occasionally dream of escaping to some solitary, remote place where it is peaceful, and, most of all, *quiet*.

Marcy's friends in the childcare association encouraged her to take a child development class at the local community college, and Marcy began to understand why her adult expectations and logic so frequently didn't "work" with the children in her care. Understanding them was far more complicated than Marcy had supposed. Truth is, young children inhabit a world very different from that of their teachers and parents. Working with young children, whether in a large childcare facility or a small in-home center, requires that teachers and childcare providers learn to get into a young child's world, to understand what they need and who they are at each stage of their young lives.

> Truth is, young children inhabit a world very different from that of their teachers and parents.

While a comprehensive study of child development is beyond the scope of this book, in this chapter we will explore the qualities that make preschoolers so fascinating—and so frustrating. Understanding "developmental appropriateness" will help you build relationships with the children in your care that are based on respect, understanding, and kindness and will help you know where to begin in managing behavior.

The Miraculous Brain: Understanding How Children Learn

OUR UNDERSTANDING OF brain growth and development—how children learn—has been revolutionized over the past few years. Not long ago, we believed that babies were born with brains that were more or less "finished"; all that remained was to fill the waiting brain with the necessary information, language, and skills. The advent of more sophisticated technology gave researchers the ability to peer into a young child's living, growing brain, and what they discovered there astonished them. It is more important than ever before that caregivers (and parents) understand the critical first three years of a child's life.

The human brain begins life as a small cluster of cells in the fetus. By the fourth week of pregnancy, these cells have begun to sort themselves out according to the function they will one day perform and have begun to "migrate" to the part of the brain they are destined to occupy. Nature provides the fetus with more cells than it will need; some do not survive the journey, while others join together in a network of connections called *synapses*.

This network continues to grow even after the baby is born. By the time a child is two years old, his brain has the same number of synapses as an adult's; by the age of three, he has more than one thousand trillion connections—twice as many as his parents and caregivers. The human brain is truly "under construction" for the first three years of life, and what a child learns and decides about himself and the world around him has a long-term influence: It becomes part of the "wiring" of his brain. By about the age of ten, a child's brain begins to prune away the synapses that haven't been used. By adolescence, half have been discarded. (Interestingly enough, even then the brain isn't complete. During adolescence, the prefrontal cortex—that part of the brain responsible for "executive functions" such as good judgment, setting priorities, and reasoning—continues to grow and may not be fully functional until a child is fifteen or sixteen. This fact may help explain why the leading cause of death among teenagers is accidents.)

> The human brain is truly "under construction" for the first three years of life, and what a child learns and decides about himself and the world around him has a long-term influence.

While the brain is amazingly flexible and able to adapt to change or injury, there are windows early in a child's life during which important learning (e.g., language development) takes place. If those windows are missed, it may become more difficult for a child to acquire those abilities. A good early childhood curriculum will take these windows of opportunity into account. Brain development is a "use it or lose it" proposition—and what is used (and kept) depends on the adults who shape a child's world.

The Dance of Nature and Nurture

WHAT SHAPES PERSONALITY? Is there really any way to shape who and what a child becomes? Much has been said and written about the influence of human genes; although they may dispute the reason or the degree, researchers generally agree that genes are an important factor in temperament and personality. For instance, genes may predispose their owner toward such characteristics as shyness, aggression, optimism, or even risk taking—which may be old news to caregivers who must forever pluck the same toddlers from the top of jungle gyms, walls, and trees.

> Brain development is a "use it or lose it" proposition—and what is used (and kept) depends on the adults who shape a child's world.

Just as important as a child's genetic inheritance is the environment he encounters as he grows. Although he inherits certain traits and tendencies from his parents, the story of how those traits develop hasn't been written yet. How you and his other caregivers interact with him will shape the person he becomes. Remember, children are always making decisions about how to find belonging, how to thrive, or how to survive. Those decisions are based on what a child encounters as he grows and are a powerful influence on his developing personality. As educational psychologist Jane M. Healy puts it, "Brains shape behavior, and behavior shapes brains."

In reality, there are few absolutes about the human mind. It is impossible to generalize about what is right or wrong for each individual child, but some scholars like Jane Healy believe that our fast-paced modern culture (and some of our "educational" television shows) may be affecting children's ability to pay attention, to listen, and to learn later in life.

We believe that children learn best in the context of *relationships,* and what they most need to learn early in life isn't found on flash cards (or on television). How their caregivers relate to them—how they talk, play, set limits, and nurture—is by far the most important factor in a young child's life.[1]

---

1. For more information on early brain growth and development, see www.iamyourchild.org; Rima Shore, *Rethinking the Brain: Research and Implications of Brain Development in Young Children* (New York: Families and Work Institute, 1997); and Jane Healy, *Endangered Minds: Why Children Don't Think and What We Can Do About It* (New York: Simon & Schuster, 1990).

Child Development and "Developmental Appropriateness"

IN THIS ENLIGHTENED day and age, most adults who work with young children have had some exposure to the principles of child development. Still, it can be remarkably easy to forget about the importance of developmental stages when you are confronted with a defiant two-year-old or an independent four-year-old. There are a number of ways to view emotional development, but we believe that the work of Erik Erikson,[2] one of the pioneers in understanding human development, continues to be one of the best ways of understanding the world of young children.

Trust Versus Mistrust: The First Year of Life

Erikson believed that the primary task during the first year of a child's life is the development of a sense of trust, particularly in parents and other caregivers—which eventually generates a sense of trust in self. A sense of trust (which is related to a sense of *attachment*) means that an infant feels or senses that she can rely on the care and support of others. To develop a sense of trust, a baby needs to have her basic needs met consistently and kindly. She needs proper nutrition, a comfortable temperature, dry diapers, adequate sleep, and lots and lots of touching, holding, and cuddling. Reliable, consistent routines can also help establish a sense of trust.

Children learn best in the context of relationships, and what they most need to learn early in life isn't found on flash cards (or on television).

A neglected baby (one whose basic needs for food, comfort, and loving touch have not been met) will develop a sense of mistrust in life and may embark on her journey through life unsure of her ability to influence what happens to her. Surprisingly, pampering may be as damaging as neglect; a baby who has never had to learn patience or self-reliance, whose every whimper results in being picked up, may also struggle with trust. More important, she may lose the ability to *self-soothe*, to gain mastery

---

2. For example, see *Childhood and Society* (New York: Norton, 1963).

To develop a sense of trust, a baby needs to have her basic needs met consistently and kindly.

of her own body and emotions and to calm herself, and may develop more manipulation skills than confidence. Babies need quiet time free from stimulation as much as they need attention.

The best solution, as in most issues involving children, is *balance*. A baby should not be left in a play pen or infant seat for too long, and a caregiver should not feel like a slave to the baby. Babies and young children need attention and care, but they also can learn from occasional discomfort in order to develop trust and confidence in themselves. Interestingly enough, children learn trust best when their caregiver has an attitude of confidence and trust.

Autonomy Versus Doubt and Shame: The Second Year of Life

Toddlers often seem like perpetual motion machines. "Why," gasped one teacher of toddlers at the end of a hectic day, "didn't God give adults as much energy as he gave children?" Toddlers are interested in and curious about everything: They want to play in the toilet, unravel the toilet paper, and splash in the sink. They want to get every toy out of the toy box, try on every article of clothing in the dress-up corner, and spread Legos all over the floor. They want your help and attention, and they want to do things by themselves. And they want to touch and investigate everything they can get their hands on.

Erikson believed that during the second year of life, young children are developing a sense of autonomy. (Notice that we said a *sense* of autonomy; they do not have, nor should they have, autonomy itself.) *Autonomy* is a child's sense that he has some power over his destiny, that his choices influence what happens to him, and that he can act upon his environment. A sense of trust developed in the first year of life and a sense of autonomy developed in the second year of life build the foundation for healthy confidence and self-esteem. Children who are not allowed opportunities to experience autonomy may develop a sense of doubt and shame instead—one excellent reason not to rely on punishment, punitive time-outs, hand slapping, and other attempts to crush or control a child's natural urge to explore.

Remember, effective discipline is respectful, works in the long term, and encourages the development of life skills and healthy attitudes. Can you recognize these two youngsters among those you care for?

Jeremy is three years old, and although his parents often laugh that he is a "handful," they delight in their son's curiosity and willingness to experiment with and explore the world around him. Jeremy's mother discovered him one bright morning making a cake in the kitchen; he had stirred milk, raisins, two eggs (with shells), Cheerios, and lots of flour in the largest bowl he could find. Jeremy's dad found him a few days later with a screwdriver and pliers, investigating the inner workings of the vacuum cleaner. Jeremy, his parents have decided, needs invitations to help in the kitchen, a set of his own small tools (and nonelectrical objects to experiment with)—and lots of supervision. Despite the occasional messes, they're happy to know that their son finds his world a fascinating and welcoming place.

> Autonomy is a child's sense that he has some power over his destiny, that his choices influence what happens to him, and that he can act upon his environment.

Matthew is also three years of age, but Matthew's world is a different sort of place than Jeremy's. Matthew is most comfortable in front of the television, watching a video. New people and places frighten him and he rarely speaks, although his parents often tell him not to be "so shy." Matthew loves the computer and tried to help his dad with his work, but something happened to Dad's files and Dad got mad. Matthew would like to work in the garden with his mom, too, but after he dug a whole row of

small holes for her to put plants in, she sighed the big sigh that Matthew hates and told him to go play in the house. It feels safer to Matthew not to have too many ideas, and when people raise their voices he hunches into a small ball. It will take some time and a lot of encouragement for Matthew to show his curiosity again.[3]

How will Jeremy and Matthew get along in their childcare center? What will their teachers need to keep in mind to provide both limits and structure and an inviting environment? How can their teachers help these two different little boys get along with others, develop confidence and self-discipline, and realize their fullest potential?

A toddler's inborn drive to develop a sense of autonomy undoubtedly is one of the primary reasons adults find toddlers so challenging. It may help to remember that toddlers do not set out to defeat or discourage you intentionally. Indeed, young children frequently are as frustrated by adults as adults are by young children; after all, adults are always messing up a child's plans and ideas. You can help the children in your care learn a healthy sense of autonomy by providing a physical environment that is inviting and safe, a range of opportunities for exploration and curiosity, time for training in valuable life skills, encouragement for the many things they *can* do, and discipline that is kind and firm. (Refer to chapter 2 and the A to Z section for specific suggestions on dealing with childcare challenges in developmentally appropriate ways.)

Initiative Versus Guilt: From Two to Six

Parker has lots of ideas. It was Parker's idea to pull up the playground fence and lead three other children on an expedition to visit a horse in the neighboring field. It was Parker's idea to "help" the plumber by turning the faucets on and off while the plumber was under the sink. And it was Parker's idea to play a joke on Miss Christy by leaping out of his cubby and shrieking just as she walked by. Parker is irrepressible, curious, inventive—and the terror of the four-year-old classroom. "I don't know what to do with him," Miss Christy frequently says—but she can't help admiring his ingenuity and energy. Still, she sometimes counts the days until his fifth birthday, when he will move into Mr. John's class.

---

3. From *Positive Discipline: The First Three Years* (Roseville, CA: Prima, 1998), p. 73.

POSITIVE DISCIPLINE TOOLS TO DEVELOP AUTONOMY

- Use kind, firm action—not words alone—to manage behavior.
- Use distraction and/or redirection to focus toddlers on acceptable activities.
- Provide lots of supervision.
- Don't expect toddlers to understand sharing or apologies.
- Create routines to teach and to ease transitions throughout the day.
- Offer limited choices.
- Ask "what" and "how" questions (see page 62) to develop language skills and invite participation and good judgment.

Erikson believed that children between the ages of two and six develop a sense of initiative. When we say that a child needs a healthy sense of initiative, we do not mean that he should be allowed to carry out every idea that pops into his head. We do mean that he needs secure boundaries and limits within which he can explore, experiment, and learn to believe in his own competence and capability. Creating a balance between safety (and appropriate behavior) and creativity and courage is the essence of working with a three-year-old.

Preschoolers see their world as a fascinating and exciting place, especially as their physical, intellectual, and social skills increase. Adults sometimes respond to a child's growing sense of initiative by making rules—lots and lots of rules—or by becoming overly protective and anxious. Either course may thwart a child's need to experience the results of her own choices and may result either in discouragement and passivity (and, as you may remember, discouraged children often misbehave) or outright rebellion and resistance.

Wise caregivers learn to allow for healthy initiative while still creating appropriate limits and boundaries. An example is every preschooler's favorite word: "No!" Most caregivers and parents would prefer that the children in

> Wise caregivers learn to allow for healthy initiative while still creating appropriate limits and boundaries.

their lives say no less often and respond more quickly to the no's that adults say. There are ways to hear no less often, and to invite cooperation from children. Here are some suggestions to consider:

- **Tell children what they can do, rather than what they can't.** For instance, instead of saying, "No throwing blocks!" you might say, "Looks like you want to do some throwing. Shall we go outside and throw the ball?"

- **Say yes instead of no.** If a child asks for a snack, you could say, "Yes—just as soon as the toys are picked up," instead of "No, you haven't picked up the toys yet." Or you can let children experiment with ideas that aren't dangerous to them. If Kevin wants to put catsup in his fruit punch, you don't have to say no; he may learn something from the experiment, and you can help him learn life skills by cleaning up his concoction afterward.

- **Remember that sometimes it is appropriate for children to say no.** All of us need to feel comfortable saying no when it is appropriate. (After all, how many times have you found yourself doing something you don't want to do because you didn't have the courage or felt too much guilt to say no?) You can let children practice in safe and respectful ways by offering them choices. No is an appropriate answer for questions like "Do you want some more juice?" or "Can Melissa give you a hug?"

Encouraging the development of initiative is a vitally important task—and one that caregivers often find challenging and inconvenient. Positive Discipline tools will help you respond to these challenges in effective ways (see the sidebar).

Other Aspects of Developmental Appropriateness

THERE ARE HUNDREDS of ways in which young children are different than adults, but remembering some of the more important ones will help you work more confidently and positively with your young charges.

POSITIVE DISCIPLINE TOOLS TO HELP DEVELOP INITIATIVE

- Ask "what" and "how" questions; don't lecture or nag.
- Establish clear, age-appropriate expectations—in advance.
- Invite cooperation and participation—and teach life skills.
- Have regular class meetings and focus on solutions.
- Offer limited choices.
- Create routines to ease transitions throughout the day.
- Use positive time-out to help children manage emotions.
- Decide what you will do and follow through with dignity and respect.

Physical Development Takes Time

There is an old child development saying that physical growth and maturity spread from the inside out and from the top down. In other words, the first parts of a healthy child's body that function efficiently are the heart and lungs; strength and control spread outward from there, reaching the fingers last. Children can move and control their heads first, while walking and eventually running happen much later. Fine-motor control—the ability to manipulate small objects and do complicated tasks with one's hands—is one of the last skills to emerge in children, which is why tasks like tying shoes can pose problems for so many youngsters.

Teachers and childcare providers usually value cooperation and obedience, and it can be tempting to confine young children physically to a small space. But to master the challenges of physical maturation, children must have safe spaces in which to climb, maneuver, and explore.

Process Versus Product

Adults like products. We like to see the proof that we've accomplished something, and we generally tend to have fixed goals in mind as we go through our busy days. Children, especially young children, see the world much differently.

Patsy Green arrived at the childcare center one afternoon just in time to see Laura Anderson and her son carrying a huge, colorful painting out to the car. Patsy looked around eagerly to see what her son Paul had painted, but none of the pictures had his name on them.

Baffled, Patsy cornered the teacher and asked why Paul hadn't had a chance to paint that day.

"Well," the teacher said, "Paul was very interested in the paint—but not in putting it on the paper. He stirred the colors and experimented with the feeling of the paint on his fingers, then decided he'd really rather build with blocks." She smiled, for she understood that Paul was interested in the process, in texture and balance and fit, not in producing a product.[4]

Although it isn't always possible to move at the leisurely pace children prefer, it can help you keep your patience and perspective to realize that children are learning as much (if not more) from the process of dabbling, poking, dropping, and gazing as they do achieving a goal or producing an object. When you must hurry, take time to explain to children why you must achieve a certain goal. Set reasonable expectations in advance, and let children know what to expect. And be sure to find other opportunities for "enjoying the moment."

Fantasy Versus Reality

Bonnie was talking to one of the other teachers when three-year-old Megan came rushing in from the playground. "Miss Bonnie, Miss Bonnie!" she called, tugging impatiently at Bonnie's jacket. "I saw a tiger behind the jungle gym!"

"Oh, Megan," Bonnie replied, shaking her head. "There are no tigers at our preschool. Don't you know it's wrong to make up stories?"

Bonnie's reaction might have been different if she'd known that Megan and her family had watched Walt Disney's *The Jungle Book* last night. Or that Megan's mother had been reading Winnie the Pooh and Tigger stories to her every afternoon. Or that one of the neighborhood cats had jumped the fence into the playground again. Tigers are very much on Megan's mind, and it isn't surprising that she "saw" one.

---

4. From *Positive Discipline for Preschoolers*, rev. 2d ed. (Roseville, CA: Prima, 1998), p. 50.

Children live in a much less literal world than do adults. They are not born understanding the difference between truth and lies, and they will not automatically value honesty. Nor do they instinctively understand that what they see on television and movie screens isn't "real"—if they can see it, they are quite likely to believe it. Fantasy and games of pretend provide a means for children to experiment with and communicate concepts they may not yet have words for, things like emotions or ethical issues.

Rather than automatically correcting children's misconceptions or scolding them for "lying," take a moment to get into their world and understand what their stories mean to them. Use "what" and "how" questions to invite them to share their perceptions with you. Above all, recognize that the ways children perceive their world are not "right" or "wrong." They are part of a child's developmental process, and entering the world through a child's unique window of vision can make all the difference in winning their cooperation.

> Fantasy and games of pretend provide a means for children to experiment with and communicate concepts they may not yet have words for.

Time

Any adult who has heard the age-old cries, "Are we there yet?" or "How long until my birthday?" understands that children perceive time much differently than do adults. For children, five minutes can be an eternity, and concepts of time (days, weeks, months, or minutes) blur together in a muddled mass.

Children may tell you with completely sincerity that they went to Disneyland "yesterday" (it was actually last month) or are having a baby brother "tomorrow" (well, seven months from now is sort of tomorrow).

Wise caregivers know that helping children deal with time can make a huge difference in their attitude. For instance, you can use visual signals to indicate time—fingers pinched close together mean "just a little time" while arms spread far apart mean "a lot of time." Or you can give a child a kitchen timer, set it, and invite her to tell you when the beeper sounds. You can focus on discipline that teaches rather than punishment that frustrates or invites defiance. Positive time-out or other Positive Discipline solutions will help children manage their behavior far better than punitive approaches such as taking away privileges "for a week" or time-out that relies on isolation and confinement for a set period of time. (What is that child on the time-out bench *really* thinking and deciding while he waits for you to let him out?) You will feel less frustration with children's approach to time when you can consider it an opportunity for learning.

> Wise caregivers know that helping children deal with time can make a huge difference in their attitude.

Temperament: Finding Goodness of Fit

YOU'VE PROBABLY HEARD it said that it isn't wise to compare one child with another, but chances are good that you (like the rest of us) have done it anyway, at least in the privacy of your own thoughts. Brian is "such a good boy," while Miranda is "a little monster" or "a spoiled brat." We usually think of "good" children as being those who cheerfully obey their caregivers and parents, don't fight with other children, share happily, help out without complaining, and generally behave like a version of the Gerber baby—charming, smiling, bright, and cute.

But as we've already seen, normal development can lead children to behave in ways that are not "good." In addition, each child's individual and unique *temperament* can present caregivers with challenges. How do you recognize and accept a child's differences, both strengths and flaws, and help that child do her best?

There are many ways of describing temperament, the qualities and characteristics that contribute to individual personality, but we have found the work of Drs. Stella Chess and Alexander Thomas particularly helpful.[5] Chess and Thomas have identified nine aspects of temperament: activity level, rhythmicity, initial response, adaptability, sensory threshold, quality of mood, intensity of reaction, distractibility, and persistence and attention span. These temperaments serve to describe three types of children: the "easy" child, the "difficult" child, and the "slow to warm up" child. All are good; some are just more challenging than others. All children possess varying degrees of each characteristic. With understanding and acceptance, parents and teachers can respond to temperament differences in ways that encourage development and growth; they also can help children reach their real potential, rather than simply trying to mold them into "good" children. You may want to think about individual children you know as we explore the nine temperaments.

> With understanding and acceptance, parents and teachers can respond to temperament differences in ways that encourage development and growth.

Activity Level

Activity level refers to a child's level of motor activity and the proportion of active and inactive periods. Some children seem never to slow down, preferring running, jumping, and climbing to quieter pursuits (this does not mean, incidentally, that they are "hyperactive"). Other children are quite content to sit with a book, a puzzle, or some crayons for long periods of time.

Understanding a child's activity level can help you plan ahead. Active children will do best when they have adequate time for energetic activities. They will not do best when forced to sit quietly. If you have lots of active youngsters in your care each day, dealing with them takes lots of energy; be sure you create ways to rest and relax yourself. It probably won't help you much to lament your fate and wish for more peaceful children. You (and the children) will do best when you thoughtfully plan for their activity level.

---

5. See their *Know Your Child* (New York: Basic Books, 1987) and other related resources.

NINE TEMPERAMENTS THAT SHAPE A CHILD'S PERSONALITY AND APPROACH TO LIFE

- Activity level
- Rhythmicity
- Initial response (approach or withdrawal)
- Adaptability
- Sensory threshold
- Quality of mood
- Intensity of reactions
- Distractibility
- Persistence and attention span

Rhythmicity

Rhythmicity refers to the predictability of biological functions such as sleeping, eating, and toileting. Nor surprisingly, highly predictable youngsters are easier to manage in group settings than those who seem to be on a different schedule each day. Life in the real world usually means, however, that you will have some regular children—and some who run on a schedule known only to themselves. Understanding that it isn't always possible to have the "right" routine for naps, snacks, meals, and toilet trips can spare you unnecessary frustration. It isn't personal; it's just rhythmicity.

> Understanding that it isn't always possible to have the "right" routine for naps, snacks, meals, and toilet trips can spare you unnecessary frustration.

Initial Response (Approach or Withdrawal)

Some children approach a new situation or person with curiosity and eagerness; others hide behind the nearest adult and watch for a while. You can usually determine a child's initial response by simply watching him: Does he smile, reach for a new toy, or go to join a new group of children, or does he cry, hide, or spit out a new food? Recent research indicates that this temperament is highly influenced by genes. Shy people tend to remain shy for life, although they certainly can learn to cope with their shyness in ways that make it easier to bear. Urging a child who instinctively withdraws from new situations to "get over it" won't help. Understanding temperamental differences can assist you in teaching limits to the child who knows no fear and encouraging the child who fears too much.

Adaptability

Adaptability describes how a child reacts to a new situation over time, his ability to adjust and change. For instance, one child may cry the first time or two that his mother leaves him with you, but will eventually get used to his new surroundings and even look forward to coming. Other children find it much harder to make this sort of transition. As with so many aspects of working with young children, it helps immensely not to take this temperament trait personally. Patience and the willingness to give a child space to adjust to new things gradually will help you both.

> As with so many aspects of working with young children, it helps immensely not to take any temperament trait personally.

Sensory Threshold

Some children are unfazed by sand in their shoes, scratchy clothing, or hot pavement; others find just about everything irritating and unsettling. The level of sensitivity to sensory input varies from one child to the next and affects how they behave and view their world. It is also one more aspect of temperament that adults just can't argue with—no matter how hard they may try. Again, understanding sensory differences will help you work with children to help them feel more comfortable in their world and to understand the effect on their behavior of the sensory input they receive. (Sensory integration dysfunction, a congenital condition that makes it difficult for children to assimilate sensory input, will be discussed in chapter 7 on special needs.)

Quality of Mood

This trait, too, appears to be highly influenced by genes. Some children are just born optimists, seeing the bright side of everything, while others see a darker world. It is important to remember that a child's optimism or pessimism, cheerfulness or sadness, are not necessarily a response to the quality of care you give him.

You can help a child explore his view of the world by asking "what" and "how" questions and listening without judgment to the answers you get. You may also invite a child to share with you his happiest and saddest moments of the day. You may discover opportunities in these conversations to assist children in seeing rainbows where there appeared to be only rainstorms.

> A child's optimism or pessimism, cheerfulness or sadness, are not necessarily a response to the quality of care you give him.

Intensity of Reaction

Some children cry for an hour over a scraped knee or shriek in fright when the telephone rings; others sniffle for a moment or two, then run off to do something new. Understanding that children react to stimuli with varying degrees of intensity can help teachers and caregivers deal with behavior more calmly.

Distractibility

It is quiet time at the childcare center when Christopher makes the discovery that his favorite stuffed animal has been left at home. The teacher talks with him, holds him, rocks him, and offers a stuffed rabbit as a consolation, but Christopher cannot be distracted; he spends the entire quiet time whimpering for his toy.

Annie, on the other hand, is upset when she first realizes that her favorite blue mat has been taken by another child. However, when her teacher offers a pretty purple one, Annie is content to settle down and rest.

It is important to realize that both Annie and Christopher's different temperaments may prove to be assets later in life. Christopher's ability to focus on one issue to the exclusion of all else may serve him well as a surgeon or researcher, while Annie's flexibility may make her a wonderful teacher someday. Recognizing the assets of each child's temperament can help you bring out that child's best.

Persistence and Attention Span

Persistence refers to a child's willingness to pursue an activity in the face of obstacles or difficulties; *attention span* describes the length of time he will pursue an activity without interruption. The two characteristics are usually related.

Kimmy will spend an entire hour trying to make a tower of blocks, regardless of how many times Matthew knocks it over; Ashley gives up in tears at the first challenge. Sarah will play with one doll all morning, while Laura has exhausted the entire contents of the toy box by snack time. These children are demonstrating the qualities of persistence and attention span. It is important to note that a short attention span does not necessarily indicate the presence of attention deficit disorder but may be a normal part of a child's inborn temperament or part of his or her natural developmental process.

There is no denying that some temperament traits are "easier" than others. Teachers and caregivers, too, have temperaments, and sometimes your temperament will not mesh easily with the temperament of a child you must care for. This does not mean that either you or the child is wrong or "bad." Chess and Thomas call this issue "goodness of fit," the ease with which a parent or teacher can get along with a particular child. Some children are an instant delight, while others are a constant challenge. Regardless, understanding development and temperament, a willingness to be both kind and firm, and using Positive Discipline skills to discover solutions will help both you and the children you care for each day to get along and to do your best.

> Teachers and caregivers, too, have temperaments, and sometimes your temperament will not mesh easily with the temperament of a child you must care for.

Development, temperament, and brain growth are complicated issues—and understanding them is critical to your ability to work well with young children. We highly encourage you to learn all you can about them. Recognizing, accepting, and appreciating the wonderful world of young children will enable you to create an encouraging and positive environment for all of you.

5

Children Together

Gender, Social Skills, and the Importance of Play

What are little girls made of?
Sugar and spice and everything nice.
That's what little girls are made of.
What are little boys made of?
Frogs and snails and puppy dog tails.
That's what little boys are made of.

—Old nursery rhyme

TAKE A LOOK around your childcare center during playtime. What do you see? Over in the corner, two little girls are waiting patiently for circle time because their teacher is going to read the next chapter in a favorite book. As they converse quietly, they lean from side to side to avoid the three little boys who are dashing madly about, playing a noisy game of tag. Over in the kitchen corner, young Sam is patiently arranging clay in muffin tins, while Cammi, his assistant, waits to put them in the oven. Keith and Kevin are having a meeting of their secret club, whose motto is "No girls allowed!" Jennifer is rattling the doorknob trying to get out to play on the jungle gym—again—while Martin is right behind her, egging her on. Meanwhile, Mary is tugging on the teacher's pant leg, repeating over and over, "Jennifer's trying to get out again. Teacher, Jennifer's trying to get *out*."

Who behaves better—the boys or the girls? Teachers and parents alike love to debate who is "easier"—boys or girls. Indeed, society has made certain

assumptions about boys and girls for hundreds of years, and those assumptions and biases are reflected in the ways we work with children, the expectations we hold for them, and our perceptions of who they are and who they might become. Most adults understand that the truth is a bit more complicated than that old nursery rhyme about sugar and spice would indicate—but how? Political correctness aside, are boys and girls really different? If they are, what are those differences? And what do teachers, caregivers, and early childhood educators need to know about gender and the way boys and girls interact with each other?

Boys and Girls: Different and the Same

THE PAST FORTY years or so have brought sweeping changes in the way society perceives gender. For many years, few people questioned that boys liked sports, guns, trucks, and rough play, while girls naturally preferred dolls, tea parties, and books. Boys would grow up to be soldiers, policemen, and doctors; girls should prepare for a life spent nurturing others, either by raising children and caring for a family or perhaps, if they were more ambitious, by becoming a nurse or a teacher. Boys were boisterous, competitive, and energetic; girls were quiet, peaceful creatures, shy, and timid and in need of protection by bigger, stronger males.

Then came the era of feminism. Suddenly it became unacceptable to make assumptions about gender, although most people couldn't help doing so.

Women could now become doctors and pilots and lawyers and were entitled to equal rights and equal pay. Men were supposed to become more "sensitive" and caring, to be more involved in raising their children, and to avoid the perils of male chauvinism. In short, no one knew for certain *how* girls and boys should behave or what their relative strengths and weaknesses might be.

So here's the news flash: Boys and girls are both the same and different. All children, regardless of gender, need a sense of belonging and significance, pass through a series of developmental stages, and do best when treated with respect, kindness, and firmness. They deserve equal opportunities in education, relationships, careers, and potential. But there is no denying that boys and girls, men and women just aren't identical, and the differences go far beyond physical appearance and genitalia. The same technology that taught us so much about brain growth and development in early childhood has revealed that boys' and girls' brains actually are structured and operate somewhat differently. Researchers now believe that these differences influence all sorts of behavior, including the rate of emotional and social development, learning styles, how boys and girls play (and with what), and certain aspects of personality.

> All children, regardless of gender, need a sense of belonging and significance, pass through a series of developmental stages, and do best when treated with respect, kindness, and firmness.

These differences are often minor, and it is important to remember that generalizing about any human being, especially on the basis of gender, is dangerous. For caregivers, though, who tend to work with children in groups, the differences between genders are an important aid to understanding how best to get into a child's world, understand him or her, and create an environment where boys and girls alike can feel welcome, encouraged, and appreciated.

Sugar and Spice or Frogs and Snails?

DURING THE MID-1970S, twin boys were born to a Canadian family. During a botched circumcision, one of the little boys' penises was burned so badly that it had to be removed. "No problem," the doctors told the distraught parents. "Simply raise him as a girl. Dress him as a girl, give him a girl's name and girls' toys; when 'she' is older, we'll start sex hormone shots and do cosmetic surgery. She won't be able to have children, but she should have a happy, normal life as a woman."

So the parents did as the doctors suggested. They raised their child as a girl, never telling anyone the true story. But something wasn't right. As the little "girl" grew, she never felt *right* in a girl's body. She wanted to play with her brother's toys and do what the other boys did. As she grew older, she was attracted to other girls, a fact that caused her untold confusion. She didn't look right, either; she was taller and thicker than the other girls and was teased incessantly. Only after the hormones and surgery had begun did her parents—against the doctors' advice—tell "her" the truth: She was really a boy.[1]

> If you work with children, your attitude toward their gender will have an influence on how they perceive their own potential.

What makes a girl "feel" and behave differently than a boy? By their second or third birthday, most children can identify their own gender. "I'm a girl," they say proudly, or "I'm a boy." They are also acutely tuned to the gender of other children and to what differentiates boys from girls, including hair, clothing, and toys. In fact, according to Susan Gilbert,[2] most two- and three-year-olds can tell you that pink and lavender are "girl" colors, while brown and blue are "boy" colors. Culture matters: Children in Holland, where gender roles are among the most flexible, hold fewer stereotypes about males and females than do children in Italy, where women are still expected to serve men. It is important to remember that if you work with children, *your* attitude toward their gender will have an influence on how they perceive their own potential.

What effect do gender differences have in a childcare setting? Let's take a brief look at the areas in which boys and girls tend to differ most. Again, we are talking about general differences between boys and girls as a *group,* not as individuals. Individual traits may form not only because they are biologically influenced but because they are reinforced, accepted, or encouraged by parents or

---

1. For more information on this fascinating case, see John Colapinto, *As Nature Made Him: The Boy Who Was Raised as a Girl* (New York: HarperCollins, 2000).

2. *A Field Guide to Boys and Girls* (New York: HarperCollins, 2000).

teachers. Still, you are likely to observe some of these traits in your childcare facility or classroom.

Energy Level

Yes, boys tend to be more physically active. Although lots of girls love to climb trees and run for hours, boys usually have more energy—and a greater need to run, climb, jump, shout, and move around. Little boys often use physical movement as part of their own process of self-exploration. Research has also found that boys are even more active when they play with other boys than when they play with girls.

The implications for childcare are clear: If you have a bunch of boys to work with, you (and they) will be very frustrated if you expect them to sit quietly all day long. Plan for physical activity and allow lots of opportunities for movement; you'll be more likely to receive their cooperation when you do need to slow down for a while.

Verbal Skills

Have you ever suggested to a child, "Use your words"? Did you know that some boys will struggle to comply simply because they are boys? As a group, boys tend to be slower to develop verbal and language skills than girls. Girls learn to use the left hemisphere of the brain, the part primarily responsible for language, earlier than do boys. Also, for reasons that no one completely understands, parents of infant boys are less likely to converse with them than are parents of infant girls, further encouraging girls to speak sooner and better than boys.

As a group, boys tend to be slower to develop verbal and language skills than girls.

In addition, boys employ a different style of communication than do girls. According to Deborah Tannen,[3] girls tend to ask, to invite, and to offer choices. Boys, on the other hand, are more likely to issue directives and commands. Because language skills have such a powerful influence on behavior, speech delays and an inability to articulate needs and feelings often result in frustration and misbehavior such as hitting, kicking, and throwing. Teachers can help by using active listening (page 61), asking "what" and "how" questions, and taking time to converse with boys as clearly and patiently as they do with girls.

Aggression and Impulse Control

Folk wisdom has told us for centuries that males are more aggressive than females. This trait may be especially reinforced by culture and environment (parents are more likely to roughhouse, tickle, and wrestle with little boys than with little girls) and by the rate at which language skills develop (girls are more likely to use words as weapons than fists or feet). Still, research tells us that aggression is also heavily influenced by genes and by gender. Yes, boys do tend to act more aggressively than do girls, to be more competitive, and to be more likely to act on impulse.

This fact is yet another good reason to avoid punitive or shaming forms of behavior management in the classroom. Punishment often invites rebellion, resistance, defiance, or sneakiness. Aggressive little boys will respond much better to kind, firm *teaching*, to encouragement, and to reasonable limits and structure. It may help you to remember that aggressive behavior is not necessarily personal—it may just be part of a youngster's developing personality. Patience and respect will help a child learn balance and cooperation.

---

3. *You Just Don't Understand: Men and Women in Communication* (New York: Ballantine, 1990).

Emotional and Social Skills

It may surprise you to learn that as infants and very young children, boys tend to be more emotionally fragile than girls—despite our assumptions that boys are "stronger" and "tougher." Girls are instinctively more social, maintaining eye contact longer than boys do almost from birth. Girls tend to be more able to self-soothe than boys; they cry less, and for shorter periods of time. And things that upset babies—harsh voices, changes in routine, lack of touch or affection—tend to upset boys more. According to Susan Gilbert, from about the age of six months to about six years, "Boys are the ones who cry, and cry for longer periods, when they're scared, upset, or frustrated. The following situations upset many boys and girls, but they seem to hit boys especially hard: separating from a parent to go to school, not getting as much attention as they want from a parent, and trying to build something and having it repeatedly fall apart."[4] Boys, incidentally, may also be more affectionate than girls, running to offer hugs and kisses to parents and favorite teachers.

> Our tendency to discourage emotional expression in boys may be one reason why they are more susceptible to depression, alcohol and drug abuse, and even suicide as they reach adolescence.

Obviously, telling a scared or lonely little boy that he shouldn't cry will not help him. In fact, a number of researchers believe that our tendency to discourage emotional expression in boys may be one reason why they are more susceptible to depression, alcohol and drug abuse, and even suicide as they reach adolescence. Boys and girls alike need help in recognizing and labeling feelings (active listening will help) and coaching in the skills of negotiating conflict and solving problems. Having regular class meetings will help both boys and girls learn problem-solving skills, empathy, and confidence.

Intelligence and Learning

Boys are smarter than girls. They're better at math and science. And they get higher scores on intelligence tests. Right? Well, not exactly. Although all of

---

4. Gilbert, *A Field Guide to Boys and Girls*, 73.

these statements were believed earlier in this century, few people today would claim that any of them are automatically true. Still, boys and girls often have different experiences at school, especially in preschool and primary elementary grades. How can teachers help both boys and girls succeed academically?

Remember, boys develop more slowly than girls in terms of language and social skills. They are more physically active and less able to sit quietly for long periods of time. And they are generally slower to develop fine-motor skills such as holding a pencil and writing clearly. It shouldn't be surprising that teachers (who are overwhelmingly female in preschools and elementary schools) often prefer to have girls in their classes and that boys instinctively recognize this fact.

Actually, boys and girls tend to score equally well on standardized intelligence tests. Boys have a distinct advantage when it comes to visual-spatial skills, particularly mental rotation—the ability to perceive objects in space and physical relationships, such as reading maps, building things, and navigation. Girls frequently test better at such skills as reading comprehension, grammar, spelling, and writing.

> Boys and girls tend to score equally well on standardized intelligence tests.

Many psychologists and researchers believe that schools (and teachers) are biased against boys. It's not hard to understand why that might be true: Girls are generally quicker to master the skills and behaviors that teachers appreciate, while boys are more likely to find themselves sitting in the administrator's office. Some psychologists worry about the "boy bashing" that is prevalent in some preschools and elementary schools: Boys are punished for doing what comes naturally, and they learn to dislike school and believe they cannot succeed. These early beliefs can be devastating and can influence the remainder of a child's educational experience.

How can caregivers and teachers help? The sidebar lists ways you can help both boys and girls achieve their fullest potential.[5]

5. For more information on the influence of gender, see Mary Pipher, *Reviving Ophelia: Saving the Selves of Adolescent Girls* (New York: Ballantine, 1994); Michael Thompson and Dan Kindlon, *Raising Cain: Protecting the Emotional Life of Boys* (New York: Ballantine, 1999); and William Pollack, *Real Boys: Rescuing Our Sons from the Myths of Boyhood* (New York: Ballantine, 1998).

"Will You Play with Me?" Practicing Social Skills

EVERY PRESCHOOL AND childcare facility is a laboratory, a busy place where growing youngsters are learning to make friends, practicing their manners, and discovering what relationships are all about. Not surprisingly, many of the everyday disputes and upsets young children experience involve other children and how they get along—or don't.

Social skills such as sharing and playing together develop through training, practice, and mistakes—especially mistakes. Parents, who rarely have more

HELPING BOYS AND GIRLS SUCCEED

- Be aware of your own beliefs about boys and girls and how you react to them in your childcare center; avoid statements such as "Boys don't cry" or "Girls should be ladylike."
- Recognize that discipline is *teaching* and that no child is born understanding social rules, language skills, or "good" behavior; kind, firm discipline is always a better choice than punishment.
- Learn to recognize and encourage each child's individual strengths and to help manage inevitable weaknesses, rather than saying "Boys will be boys" or "Girls are easier."
- Provide opportunities for physical activity for both boys and girls.
- Practice language skills every day. Use active listening, "what" and "how" questions, and lots of conversation to encourage the growth of verbal skills.
- Let girls practice their strength-building; let boys practice nurturing.
- Provide a good mix of toys and allow children free access to all of them.
- Learn to see the ways children are unique as well as the ways they are the same.

> Social skills such as sharing and playing together develop through training, practice, and mistakes—especially mistakes.

than a few children to cope with at any one time, can afford to take some time to let social skills develop. For teachers and caregivers, however, who work with children in active, noisy groups, social skills are crucially important. How much easier would your workday be if all the children in your care got along, shared well, took turns, and treated each other with courtesy and kindness?

Okay, you can stop daydreaming now. The reality is that social skills, like most other forms of development, happen over time, and happen best when adults can teach, encourage, model—and have a little patience.

Understanding the Process

During their early years, young children are "egocentric." That is, children are the center of their own universe, and everything in that universe revolves (or should) around them. Toddlers see everything as "mine," not because they are selfish but because their world has not yet expanded enough to include others in any real way. Every toy a toddler sees is "mine"; the teacher's lunch may be "mine." "Share with Johnny," we tell him. But the truth is, in their early years sharing is an act that is foreign to children. In fact, when children

are between one and two years of age, they do not truly interact with each other. They either play alone, or they engage in what is called "parallel play"; they play *near* other children, side-by-side but not actually *with* them.

Eventually, children become curious about each other; they cruise up to one another and engage in active exploration. The poking, pulling, and touching that may result is not actually misbehavior, although adults certainly need to supervise these encounters and teach respect and kindness; rather, children are actively discovering that the world contains *other children*. Eventually, they will grow to recognize that these "others" also have needs, feelings, and opinions and to treat others with respect. They will learn the rudiments of friendship. But the process isn't always easy or painless.

> In their early years sharing is an act that is foreign to children.

Sharing in the Real World

Adults value sharing. We encourage children to share and sometimes scold them when they don't. But sharing is actually a complicated process that requires maturity and skill. (See page 182 for more on sharing.) Let's take a look at sharing in a two-year-old classroom:

Susie and Tommy are playing in the block area when Susie grabs the toy car that Tommy has just picked up. Both children begin to yell, "It's mine! Give it to me!" Naturally, the uproar draws the attention of Mrs. McGee, the children's teacher. She walks over and gently takes the car.

"Susie," she asks, "do you want to play with this car?" "I want it," Susie agrees firmly. Mrs. McGee turns to Tommy. "Are you playing with the car, Tommy?" Tommy's lower lip juts out a bit as he says, "It's mine."

Mrs. McGee places the car in Tommy's hands and turns to Susie. "Susie, what do you think you could say to Tommy if you want to play with the car?" "I want to play with it?" Susie offers (with only a little sulk in her voice). Mrs. McGee agrees that's one way to ask. She suggests that Susie could also try saying, "May I play with the car?"

Tommy has been watching this exchange with interest. When his teacher asks him what he might say to Susie when she asks for the car, he responds right away. "Here, you can have it," he replies, handing the car to Susie. Mrs. McGee smiles. "It's nice of you to share, Tommy. What might you say if you weren't finished with the car?"

This is a new thought for Tommy. The teacher has made it clear that just asking may not be enough. She is helping Tommy learn that he has some options and can assert his own needs, but Tommy is momentarily baffled.

Mrs. McGee turns to Susie. "Can you think of something Tommy can say, Susie?" Susie has just the answer. "He could say, 'In a minute.'" Mrs. McGee nods. "That's a good idea. Perhaps he could say that he will give it to you in ten minutes. Would that work, Tommy?" Tommy nods, and Mrs. McGee encourages him to practice saying "I'm not done yet" to Susie.[6]

> There is no substitute for understanding that respect, kindness, and good manners take time to learn and that investing that time will benefit both you and the children you care for.

Mrs. McGee is teaching both children the value of respect (both for self and others) and helping them learn to use words to express their needs, rather than grabbing or hitting. Obviously, this process takes time and patience—more time than many busy teachers and caregivers care to spend. It is important to remember that this sort of training must be repeated over and over as the developmental process continues. There is no substitute for understanding that respect, kindness, and good manners take time to learn and that investing that time will benefit both you and the children you care for.

Friendships and Other Special Relationships

Karen Foster is in the kitchen preparing lunch for the children she cares for in her home when five-year-old Amy enters in tears. "Amy, you look so sad!" Karen says kindly. "What happened?"

"Shannon and Ava won't let me play with them," Amy moans between sniffles. "Ava's supposed to be my best friend, but she invited Shannon to come home with her today. It's not fair!"

---

6. From Jane Nelsen, Cheryl Erwin, and Duffy, *Positive Discipline: The First Three Years* (Roseville, CA: Prima, 1998), p. 169.

Karen leans down, gives Amy a warm hug, and invites her to help serve the sandwiches and juice. She knows that by tomorrow, the social hierarchy among Amy, Ava, and Shannon will have rearranged itself and life will continue.

As children grow older and more mature, they will enter the world of friendships. They will eagerly search for a "best friend" and will wrestle with the inevitable hurt feelings and disappointments that come when that friend eats lunch or enjoys recess with someone else. By the age of five, children are able to play sophisticated games of dress-up or "let's pretend" and have a good working knowledge of courtesy and mutual respect—not that they always follow those rules, of course.

Social skills do not come without practice—and mistakes. Children who are successful at social relationships share several qualities: They are usually good at reading the nonverbal communication of their peers (facial expression, tone of voice, not standing too close to another child, etc.) and at sending appropriate nonverbal messages themselves. Children who struggle to fit in sometimes do not realize that while their words say, "I want to play with you," their face and body say something else altogether.

> Children who struggle to fit in sometimes do not realize that while their words say, "I want to play with you," their face and body say something else altogether.

Young children almost always respond first to nonverbal messages. You can help children recognize the messages they send by practicing with them, making faces and laughing together about the feelings they express. Or you can watch a movie or television program with the volume turned off and make guesses about what the characters are feeling.[7]

Children who form friendships with ease also tend to be good at creating roles for themselves in others' play. They can watch a game in progress for a while and offer to play a part that blends in smoothly with the other children. Children who bounce into the middle of a game and say, "Can I play?" may be met with "No" because the other children are simply too involved to create space for a newcomer.

---

7. For more information about helping children with nonverbal cues, see Stephen Nowicki, Jr. and Marshall P. Duke, *Helping the Child Who Doesn't Fit In* (Atlanta: Peachtree, 1992).

> You can use class meetings to teach gentle lessons about kindness, inclusion, and respect.

Teachers can help with this awkward and sometimes painful process by listening well, using active listening, and asking "what" and "how" questions to help children understand the effect their words and behavior have on their peers. You can use class meetings to teach gentle lessons about kindness, inclusion, and respect. Remember, children need a sense of belonging and significance, not only from adults but also from their peers. Helping each child in your care feel a sense of belonging and learn from his social missteps will make your childcare center a warmer and more welcoming place.

The Importance of Play

IT'S BEEN SAID many times: Play is a child's work. But you may be surprised to know just how much "work" and learning are happening as children build towers, paint pictures, play house or school, and ride scooters. A child at play is discovering her own physical abilities, both gross-motor skills (climbing, running, jumping) and fine-motor skills (working puzzles, stacking blocks, painting). She is learning cooperation with others and figuring out how things work. And she is exploring her imagination and creativity, learning new ideas and finding ways to solve problems.

Most adults are inclined to provide lots of structure and planned activities for children, but children often benefit most from "free play," unstructured time spent alone or in the company or their friends to climb, build, stack, pretend, and experiment. How you organize play times and materials in your childcare facility has a significant impact on how children will feel and behave in your care.

The Physical Setting

Whether you work in a large facility or care for children in your home, providing the right physical setting will make life considerably easier. Yes, you should childproof: There should be no exposed electrical cords or outlets, nor should there be small or fragile objects around that could be swallowed or broken. Toys can be displayed on low shelves, easy for a child to reach. Mirrors on the walls can be very entertaining—if they're made of nonbreakable materials. It is important that toilets, sinks, tables, and chairs are child sized or, if this is not possible, that safe access is available in the form of potty seats, stools, and small stepladders.

> Children often benefit most from "free play," unstructured time spent alone or in the company or their friends to climb, build, stack, pretend, and experiment.

Cleanliness is important, too. When many children handle toys and equipment each day, it is important to use a cleaning solution regularly to avoid contamination or infection. Changing tables and toys should all be cleaned daily, if possible. You should have health policies in place (can parents bring children who are ill?) and have an emergency preparedness program that is familiar to all staff members. Staff should also have first aid and CPR training.[8]

Toys to Grow On

Active, imaginative children can fill hours with an old computer box, a stack of plastic containers, or the cans from the pantry. Still, providing age-appropriate toys that encourage the development of skills, autonomy, and initiative will

8. For more detailed information on the physical setting of your center, see the National Association for the Education of Young Children Web site, www.naeyc.org.

allow children to learn, as well as have lots of fun. The sidebar offers some tips for picking toys for your center.

Keeping several types of toys available to children will increase both learning and enjoyment. Here are some suggestions:

Hands-on toys. Rattles, squeeze toys, balls, measuring cups and spoons, puzzles, beads, and board games build hand-eye coordination, encourage ideas about how things work, and foster cooperation and problem solving.

Books and recordings. Select brightly colored board books for young children; older children will enjoy books with colorful pictures and stories about nature, people, history, and activities. Nursery rhymes teach the rhythms and patterns of language. You may want to make a tape player available for older children and allow them to listen to music or to books-on-tape. Better yet, read aloud as part of your daily routine.

Art materials. Provide large sheets of blank paper (your local newspaper may make roll ends of newsprint available at no charge), markers, paints, safety scissors, glitter, old magazines, glue, and other materials. Children usually enjoy their own work best, so there is no need to buy expensive coloring books with preprinted pictures. A favorite art project is using glue to make collages of just about anything (junk art): buttons, pebbles, macaroni, rick-rack, fabric pieces (and other odds and ends from a sewing box), leaves, magazine pictures, and so on.

Providing age-appropriate toys that encourage the development of skills, autonomy, and initiative will allow children to learn, as well as have lots of fun.

Be sure art time happens on small tables or on a tile or linoleum floor, or put down a large drop cloth. Children can wear old shirts to cover their clothing. Use spills and messes as an opportunity to teach life skills; even mops and sponges can provide a worthwhile learning experience!

Construction toys. Blocks and building sets are perennial favorites. Children older than four or five can enjoy woodworking or tool sets, pounding nails with large heads into blocks of soft wood. Lumberyards and home supply outlets are often willing to provide scraps of lumber for children to "build" with.

Experimental materials. Children love toys they can control and create with. Sand, water, and clay provide tactile stimulation, and musical instruments

TOY BASICS: SELECTING TOYS WISELY

Toys for your childcare facility should meet the following criteria:

- They should be well constructed, with no sharp edges, splinters, or parts that pinch.
- They should be painted with nontoxic, lead-free paint or made of durable plastic.
- They should be shatterproof.
- They should be easy to clean.
- They should not be electric or battery-operated, especially for very young children.
- They should be checked frequently for safety.
- They should be age-appropriate, kept within reach only of children who are able to play safely with them.

allow children to enjoy producing sounds and "music." (Be sure to keep anything a child blows into scrupulously clean.) Pounding drums and toy pianos may drive you a bit crazy, but the noise may be worth it if the result is a budding Mozart.

Active play equipment. Children of all ages need space and equipment to build their muscles and meet physical challenges. Jungle gyms, swings, slides, scooters, and rocking toys will fill many hours with active play. Be sure toys are scaled for a child's age and size; provide adequate supervision, but don't overprotect children. They need the opportunity to experiment with their bodies and to learn confidence. If you have an in-home center and your play equipment is limited, make an effort to visit parks and playgrounds regularly. There is no substitute for active, outdoor play.

Imaginative play objects. Children love to enter the world of fantasy and stay there a while. Provide old clothes, hats, shoes, jewelry, old calculators or phones, and other "grown-up" items for children to use as they learn about the world of adults by imitation. Children will also enjoy dolls, stuffed animals, puppets, cars, and other objects that encourage them to experiment with new behaviors and ideas. Try to avoid toys or figures based on television programs or movies; children tend to act out predetermined story lines with these toys, rather than using their own creativity and imagination.[9]

A Word About "Screen Time"

CAREGIVERS OFTEN ASK about the wisdom of providing computers, videos, televisions, video games, and other technotoys. Children almost always benefit more from active play with the sorts of objects suggested earlier. Most children have more than enough exposure to television and videos at home; they do not need more in the hours they spend at childcare. The American Academy of Pediatrics recommends no television at all (that's right: absolutely none) for children under the age of two. Some brain researchers believe that screen time before the age of eight can have a negative effect on brain development. There is no doubt that, despite the abundance of educational software, children are in far greater need of active play, social skills training, and interaction and conversation with other children and caring adults than more time spent in front of a screen.

> Most children have more than enough exposure to television and videos at home; they do not need more in the hours they spend at childcare.

Watching television and videos is essentially a passive activity; little or no critical thinking is going on in the mind of a young child propped in front of the tube. Even so-called educational programs may not be helpful; the frantic, flashy format common to children's programs does not encourage sustained attention, and some studies indicate that children begin school expecting entertainment and special effects like those they see on the screen and are bored by classroom teaching. Many teachers report that attention spans, comprehension, and language skills are declining rapidly.

---

9. For more suggestions on age-appropriate toys, see *Toys: Tools for Learning*, Order 571 (Washington, D.C.: National Association for the Education of Young Children, 1999).

Computer skills are undoubtedly an important part of life in our society, and offering training and opportunities to children can be valuable—after they are eight years old.[10]

Children can certainly present many challenges, and teaching and caring for them will undoubtedly have moments of frustration for even the most committed, compassionate teacher. Still, understanding the fascinating world of young girls and boys, the ways they play and work together, and the marvelous human potential they embody makes each moment of time and effort well worthwhile.

---

10. For more information on play and toys in the childcare center, see Martha B. Bronson, *The Right Stuff for Children Birth to 8: Selecting Play Materials to Support Development* (Washington, D.C.: National Association for the Education of Young Children, 1995). See also the many resources available from the NAEYC at www.naeyc.org, as well as the American Academy of Pediatrics, www.aap.org, and the Consumer Product Safety Commission, www.cpsc.gov.

Computer skills are undoubtedly at important . . . . reading,
and offering training and opportunities to child . . . . when
they are eight years old.[19]

6

The Magic of
Encouragement

ENCOURAGEMENT IS A magical tool. Why? Because, as we have said, *a misbehaving child is a discouraged child.* Read the italicized part of the last sentence again. Think about that statement. If a misbehaving child is a discouraged child, what is the most obvious way to stop the misbehavior? It's simple: encouragement.

In the real estate community, there are three important things to consider when purchasing property: location, location, and location. You will be very successful with children in your care if you remember that the three most important things to consider for discipline are encouragement, encouragement, and encouragement.

In real estate, the importance of location makes perfect sense. However, with discipline, the idea that encouragement will affect behavior (and misbehavior) goes contrary to conventional wisdom. Conventional wisdom tells us that encouragement rewards and reinforces misbehavior. But Positive Discipline takes you far beyond conventional wisdom to a deep understanding of what motivates misbehavior and what *encourages* appropriate behavior.

> If a misbehaving child is a discouraged child, what is the most obvious way to stop the misbehavior? It's simple: encouragement.

In chapter 3, we explained the primary reason for misbehavior—a sense of not belonging. We also explained the many directions misbehavior might take (the four mistaken goals of misbehavior) when children don't feel they belong.

THE THREE ELEMENTS (OR GOALS) OF ENCOURAGEMENT

1. To create a sense of belonging
2. To create a sense of capability through the development of life skills
3. To instill a sense of social interest

We provided suggestions (tools) for discipline and will provide many more throughout this book. What we want to emphasize in this chapter is that all Positive Discipline methods have a foundation of encouragement. This foundation is established through the three elements of encouragement. When all of these elements are present, encouragement not only stops misbehavior, it imbues children with a healthy self-concept and the skills they need to make a difference in the world while living happy, productive lives.

The three elements of encouragement are essential to help children develop into well-balanced citizens of the world—and of your childcare facility.

> The three elements of encouragement are essential to help children develop into well-balanced citizens of the world—and of your childcare facility.

Having only one without the other two could create problems. Suppose a child feels a sense of belonging but doesn't feel capable or have social interest. This child may be very self-centered and demand undue attention and undue service. This is why praise can be very unhealthy. (The difference between praise and encouragement will be explained later.) A child with a sense of capability and life skills but without a sense of belonging and social interest may use those skills for revenge (against others) or for completely selfish interests. A child with social interest but lacking in the first two elements may be too unselfish and may run the risk of becoming an "approval junkie" or a self-sacrificing people pleaser.

Encouragement in Real Life

WHAT DOES ENCOURAGEMENT look like in real life when a child is misbehaving? What do you do when a child is being obnoxious, disrespectful, demanding, won't mind, is having a temper tantrum, or is hurting others? When you look at the Topics A to Z section, you will find suggestions for all of these misbehaviors and many more. In this chapter we want to emphasize encouragement tools that will work in many situations.

Encourage Yourself

Have you ever noticed how difficult it is to see a misbehaving child as a discouraged child? At these times it is not easy to remember that the child who is acting unlovable may be the child most in need of love. You may need to take some positive time-out for yourself until you calm down and can think more rationally. It is okay to share your feelings: "I'm very upset right now. I'm going to take some positive time-out until I feel better." What a great model for children. Just like children, when *you* feel better, you'll do better. After you feel better, you can get back to the child and try some of the many discipline suggestions in this book.

> You may need to take some positive time-out for yourself until you calm down and can think more rationally.

Break the Code of the Misbehavior

It isn't easy to see a misbehaving child as a "discouraged child," especially when you get emotionally hooked by the misbehavior. The child seems just plain obnoxious and not interested in belonging at all. It takes maturity, being healthy yourself, and having an understanding of human behavior to break out of the cycles of undue attention, power struggles, revenge cycles, and the hopelessness of assumed inadequacy. Every adult who has understood this and tried the tools of encouragement has found them rewarding for herself and for the child.

So, even though it isn't easy to encourage a misbehaving child because you become emotionally hooked, sooner or later you can remember that the child is trying to tell you something with his misbehavior. Look at the Mistaken

Goals Chart (page 40) for clues about how to break the code. Then focus on the last column of the chart for ideas about how to encourage. Let's explore some of those encouragement tools in greater detail.

"I need your help."

It is very encouraging to feel needed, and involving a child in the helping process teaches all three elements of encouragement. Saying "I need your help" to the child who is seeking undue attention is a great way to redirect the child into getting attention in a useful way. Saying "I need your help" to the child who is seeking misguided power is an effective way to step out of the power struggle while inviting the child to use his power in cooperative ways.

For the mistaken goals of revenge and assumed inadequacy, you have to do something first before asking for help. The child who is seeking revenge won't hear your appeal for help until she feels validated for her hurt feelings. However, once that is done, the child is usually very receptive to helping—and feels more belonging by doing so. The child who has given up (assumed inadequacy) needs help with small steps to accomplish a task first. Then, imagine how capable this child could feel by helping you or another child. (One of the reasons class meetings are so effective is that they get all the children involved in helping each other. Now, *that* is powerful.)

Hugs

Little Bobby was refusing to pick up the blocks—again. Mr. Senter felt like telling him to go sit on a chair "and think about how mean you are. See if I'll ever do anything for you, you little creep." Instead, Mr. Senter took a deep breath to calm himself, sat down next to Bobby, and said, "I need a hug. Would you be willing to give me one?"

Bobby looked shocked and confused; this was certainly not what he expected. But when Mr. Senter invitingly opened his arms, Bobby gave him a hug. It was a stiff hug for a few seconds, but pretty soon they were bear-wrestling on the floor.

Bobby was surprised again when Mr. Senter asked, "Okay, now what ideas do you have for the fastest way to get these blocks picked up?" Bobby was used to being told to put the blocks away—a sure-fire invitation to resistance from him. This question invited him to think of a way to use his power in a useful way. His reply was, "We could have a race." They did—and the blocks were put away in fifteen seconds.

Hugs are a powerful distraction from negativity, but they are even more powerful in creating that sense of belonging that all children need. A hug can create the positive learning environment that is required to invite cooperation.

It is wise to *ask* a child whether he would like a hug before touching him. Children should always have the power to control who touches their bodies, when, and how. You can tell a child, "I'd like to give you a hug—is that okay?" Or you can invite him to hug you, as Mr. Senter did with Bobby.

Will hugs (or any other single tool, for that matter) always work? Of course not. Nothing works all the time. That is why we need so many different ways to encourage those around us. Bobby could have refused to give Mr. Senter a hug. Then Mr. Senter could say, "Okay, but as soon as you are ready, I sure need a hug." Then he could walk away. Many adults who have role-played a child in this situation have shared that they have a feeling of empowerment. They didn't have to give the hug right away, but it was nice to know they had the option, and it was difficult to hang on to negative behavior after having that option.

> Hugs are a powerful distraction from negativity, but they are even more powerful in creating that sense of belonging that all children need.

Special Time

Choose the child who is the most challenging to you. Find a way to spend a few minutes of special time with that child. Perhaps you sit close to her when she first arrives in your childcare center so you can ask her, "What was the most fun thing you did yesterday?" Then share your most fun thing from the day before. Maybe you ask her to help you greet the other children with a handshake. You could tell her you are saving the chair next to you so she can sit with you at lunch.

> Even a few minutes a day of special time can reassure a child that she does belong and make misbehavior far less appealing to her.

You may be surprised at how much this special time can change her behavior—until you remember that a misbehaving child is a discouraged child because she doesn't feel a sense of belonging and significance. Even a few minutes a day of special time can reassure a child that she *does* belong and make misbehavior far less appealing to her.

Get the Child Involved

Sandy is a single parent who runs a childcare program in her home. Her own discouragement (and that of her sons) almost caused her to give up work that she loved. The following story[1] shows how using the tools of encouragement helped Sandy solve her problem.

Sandy has two children of her own, four-year-old Kyle and six-year-old Joey. Sandy told her parenting group that she needed help. Near tears, she shared that Joey was driving her crazy while she tried to manage the childcare program. "He taunts the younger children, hits them, takes their toys, and uses nasty language. He fights with the older boys over the use of the equipment. Joey's not having this trouble at school or at other friends' homes. He only misbehaves with me. He's so bad that I want to stop having the children come right now and give him the attention he needs. I think the daycare is too hard for him to handle because I'm a single mom and he doesn't want to share me with so many other kids. He's constantly saying I'm unfair."

Sandy continued to share: She had told Joey she would stop taking care of other children in June. She couldn't stop sooner because of her obligations to the families who counted on her and because she needed the money to help

---

1. From Jane Nelsen, Cheryl Erwin, and Carol Delzer, *Positive Discipline for Single Parents*, rev. 2d. ed. (Roseville, CA: Prima, 1999), pp. 113–118.

support her family. She hadn't figured out how she would earn money when she gave up childcare, but Joey was her primary concern.

The parenting group facilitator asked, "Do you want to give up your childcare business?"

Sandy answered, "No, I love it; but Joey is more important. I want peace and harmony between us, and I worry about his self-esteem."

The facilitator smiled. "Would you be willing to look at some possibilities that could help you continue providing childcare, create peace and harmony between you and Joey, and improve his self-esteem?"

Sandy didn't hesitate. "Of course I would!"

"Okay, then," said the facilitator. "Let's look at some basics first, then we'll work on some suggestions. Is it fair that you should have to stop your child care because Joey can't handle it? Could you do this without some hidden resentment?"

Sandy thought a moment. "No, probably not. I just don't know what else to do."

"Who is in control if you do give up your childcare, when you don't want to?" the facilitator asked.

"Well, obviously Joey is." Sandy shrugged. "I know that isn't healthy, but I don't know what else to do. He obviously needs my attention."

The facilitator continued, "What message are you sending to Joey by allowing him to manipulate you with his emotions?"

Now Sandy smiled wearily. "That he can be a total tyrant—and that's what it feels like to me. I'm so confused. I love him and want to be a good mother, but I will feel resentful if I give in to him and give up a job I love and can do at home. Having a daycare program in my home seemed like a perfect way to earn money without having to leave my kids. But the dream has turned into a nightmare. I don't know what to do."

The facilitator turned to the group. "It's time for some brainstorming. Let's see how many ideas we can come up with that could help Sandy and Joey."

The group came up with a long list of ideas Sandy could try. She was invited to choose the one she would feel most comfortable with. Sandy heard so many good ideas, however, that she chose a combination of several of them:

- Meet with Joey at a calm time and use the Four Steps for Winning Cooperation, which are explained in the following text.

- Let Joey have some things that he doesn't have to share with anyone.

- Spend special time alone with Joey (and with Kyle).

- Give Joey some jobs so he can feel like he is making an important contribution and also can earn some extra money.

- Get Joey involved in finding solutions to problems so he will feel he belongs and is significant.

- Reach out for support by talking to someone in a similar situation who can share his or her experience.

Sandy started with the last suggestion. She called Betty from the local childcare association and shared her problem. Betty laughed and said, "Am I ever glad I'm over that one! I had the same problem when my kids were younger. I think it's very normal—it's hard for kids to share their moms, even when they aren't single moms. Two things helped me. I wouldn't play the 'no fair' game, so my kids didn't hook me on that one. But I did allow them to have toys that were their own and didn't have to be shared with anyone. The other thing was letting them know how much I enjoyed making a good living while still being with them. It helped them to see the benefits as well as the problems."

THE FOUR STEPS FOR WINNING COOPERATION

- Get into the child's world and make a guess about what he or she might be feeling. (If you are wrong, guess again.)

- Show understanding. (Sometimes it helps to describe a time when you felt the same way.)

- Ask the child whether he or she is willing to listen to your feelings. (Children listen better when they have agreed.)

- Work on a solution together. (The first two steps create a feeling of closeness and trust, so children are willing to listen and to work on solutions in a cooperative manner.)

By talking to Betty, Sandy felt validated for her desire to make a living that included spending time with her boys. She felt encouraged in her belief that it was a worthwhile endeavor. Betty had made enough money to stay home with her children and even enough to help put them through college. "Of course," Betty added, there were some problems and hassles, but what job *doesn't* include some problems? The benefits far outweighed them."

By reaching out for support, Sandy had experienced the importance of filling her own cup—getting strength and encouragement—before she could fill Joey's cup and resolve the problem. She was able to work with Joey on positive solutions because she was able to let go of her misplaced guilt. Now that she was ready, Sandy decided to start with the Four Steps for Winning Cooperation (see the sidebar on the previous page).

Sandy was glad to see that Joey was still awake when she got home from her parenting group. Kyle had fallen asleep. It was a perfect, calm time to try the Four Steps for Winning Cooperation. Sandy started by asking Joey, "Honey, could we have a special talk just between me and you while I'm tucking you into bed?"

"Well, okay," Joey replied.

Sandy continued, "I was wondering if you feel like you aren't important to me when I'm taking care of so many other children?"

Sandy had struck a nerve. Joey replied with some heat, "It's not fair that I have to share all my stuff!"

Now Sandy reflected and validated his feelings. She offered her understanding—and a story of her own. "I can see how you'd feel that way. I can remember when I was a little girl and my mom made me share all my clothes with my younger sister, even my favorites. I hated it. I can see now that by trying to be fair to all the other kids, I was very unfair to you. I made you share your dinner-time chair, even when you tried to tell me you didn't think it was fair. I'm so sorry I didn't consider your feelings. I'll try to do better from now on, Joey."

Joey felt understood. He was touched by his mother's admission, and he started to cry. "I'm sorry for being so bad." (Children often cry from relief when they feel understood. Also, when an adult takes responsibility for disrespectful behavior, it frees children to do the same.)

Sandy reassured Joey. "Honey, you aren't bad. We both made some mistakes. I'll bet we can work on some solutions together. First, would you be willing to hear some of my feelings?"

Joey sniffled. "Okay," he said.

Sandy drew Joey close to her. "You are more important to me than any job. And I would really like to keep doing childcare so I don't have to go to work outside our home. I like being able to work and be with you at the same time. Would you be willing to help me find some ways that we can do this? I know you have some great ideas that I haven't listened to before. I'd really like to hear them now."

Joey grinned. "Okay!"

Together, Sandy and Joey came up with the following plans: Joey and Sandy would spend fifteen minutes of special time together every day, with no phones, no little brother, and no other children. Joey agreed that Kyle should have the same amount of time and that they could all work together to agree on the times that would be convenient. During a family meeting they would brainstorm suggestions for what each could do while the other was spending special time with Mom.

Joey was enthusiastic about the possibility of helping out and earning some extra money. They agreed that he would earn one dollar every day by making all the lunches for the daycare children. He volunteered to take on other jobs, like picking up toys and sweeping the floor. They also decided that no one else could sit in his dinnertime chair unless he gave permission. They ended their talk by agreeing that in the future, if something was bothering them, they would talk about it and work together on solutions that felt respectful to everyone.

> Children are never bad—but they are often discouraged.

Sandy was ecstatic at her next parenting group. "I can't believe how well this stuff works. Joey is now helping and seems to feel great about himself instead of misbehaving. At our family meeting he told Kyle how lucky they are to have a mom who can work at home. When I got Joey involved in problem solving, he had so many good ideas. I'm so glad I got to tell him how much I love him and that he could really hear me. Thank you all so much!"

Sandy found a way to get out of the win-or-lose struggle. It would not be healthy for Joey to "win" at Sandy's expense or for Sandy to "win" at Joey's expense. Control is not an issue when we learn to "win" cooperation *with* children.

Both adults and children sometimes believe that children are being "bad." Children are never bad—but they are often discouraged. And when they are discouraged, they misbehave.

The Difference Between Praise and Encouragement

EVERYONE KNOWS ABOUT the importance of praise. Parents everywhere have "One Hundred Ways to Praise a Child" posted on their refrigerators; they offer praise about their child's every action, post artwork on every available wall, and believe that in doing so, they are building their child's self-esteem. But praise—especially praise that is insincere or overdone—can lead children to become people pleasers and approval junkies, people who believe they are acceptable only when someone else is telling them they are.

Encouragement, as the word suggests, is the effort to inspire a child with courage, the courage to do the right thing whether or not Mom, Dad, or the teacher is looking. The root word of *courage* is the French word *coeur,* or heart. En-courage actually means "to *give* heart to." Dis-courage literally means to "take away heart from." The child who is encouraged is the child who has developed the internal courage to make decisions because they are the *right* decisions, a character quality also known as *integrity.* Isn't this what parents want for their children as they come face to face with the many temptations the world places before them?

> Praise—especially praise that is insincere or overdone—can lead children to become people pleasers and approval junkies, people who believe they are acceptable only when someone else is telling them they are.

Praise looks to the person: "You are such a good girl for cleaning up the lunch table." Encouragement looks to the effort: "I can tell that you worked very hard at organizing your cubby. Thank you—you must feel good about that." Praise looks to the number of A's on the report card. Encouragement looks to what was learned. Praise leads to dependence on others. Encouragement leads to self-confidence, self-reliance, and ultimately, true self-esteem. (See the following chart.)

Differences Between Praise and Encouragement[2]

	Praise	Encouragement
Dictionary Definition	1. To express a favorable *judgment* of 2. To glorify, especially by attribution of *perfection* 3. An expression of approval	1. To *inspire* with courage 2. To spur on; *stimulate*
Recognizes	Only complete, perfect product	Effort and improvement
Attitude	Patronizing, manipulative	Respectful, appreciative
"I" message	Judgmental: "I like the way you are sitting."	Self-disclosing: "I appreciate your cooperation."
Used most often with	Children: "You're such a good little girl."	Adults: "Thanks for helping."
Examples	"I'm proud of you for getting an A in math." (robs person of ownership of own achievement)	"That A reflects your hard work." (recognizes ownership and responsibility for achievement)
Invites	People to change for others	People to change for themselves
Locus of control	External: "What do you think?"	Internal: "What do I think?"
Teaches	What to think	How to think
Goal	Conformity: "You did it right."	Understanding: "What do you think/feel/learn?"
Effect on self-esteem	Feel worthwhile only when others approve	Feel worthwhile without the approval of others
Long-range effect	Dependence on others	Self-confidence, self-reliance

Adults sometimes believe that they can "give" children self-esteem by praising them, but as we have learned, this sometimes backfires. Self-esteem actually grows out of life skills, what are sometimes called *competency experiences.* Can you remember a time when a child in your care tried something new, perhaps tying his shoes or pouring his own milk, and succeeded at it?

---

2. This is based on a chart by parent educators and parenting class leaders Bonnie G. Smith and Judy Dixon of Sacramento, California.

How did he feel? One of the hidden blessings of inviting children to share responsibilities and teaching them the skills to do so is that you are building their own sense of confidence and competence in a way mere words never can. Self-esteem cannot be "given"; it must be grown within the heart of each child.

The encouraged child will make choices about life and relationships based on his or her belief that those choices are the right ones to make. The child who has been raised to expect praise for doing the right thing will become confused and discouraged when the choices he or she makes are not met with praise.

> Self-esteem cannot be "given"; it must be grown within the heart of each child.

The Joy of Social Interest

ALFRED ADLER BELIEVED that in all human beings lies the desire to contribute, to give to others, and to make our homes, our communities, and our world better places. Consider the following examples, drawn from recent newspaper articles:

- In the wake of the terrorist attacks of September 11, 2001, children across the nation sold lemonade, red-white-and-blue ribbons, and collected money in firemen's boots. They sent their dollars to the American Red Cross to help victims of the attacks.

- Classmates of a young boy undergoing treatment for cancer that caused all his hair to fall out shaved their own heads and proudly had their picture taken with their friend, bald heads shining in the sunlight.

- Children in an elementary school classroom "adopted" the residents of a local nursing home. They shared artwork, sang songs, brought cookies, and spent time each week visiting their elderly friends.

For all of these children, the only "reward" was the joy of giving to someone else. Encouragement is not just something to be received; it is something to be given away and shared. Even the youngest child can find ways to help someone else, to offer a hug or a smile, to share a cookie, or to help with a task. There may be no better way of building belonging and character than learning to give.

There are undoubtedly opportunities in your childcare facility for children to learn social interest. They can help you; they can help each other. And they can find ways to make the community they live in a better place. Perhaps you can clean up trash along your street, plant flowers in a park, or visit a hospital or nursing home. You can brainstorm with children in a class meeting about ways to help others. Finding ways to reach out not only builds self-esteem and teaches life skills but also creates a sense of belonging and empowerment in the world that all of us must share.

> Encouragement is not just something to be received; it is something to be given away and shared.

As you look at all the Positive Discipline tools we suggest, you will see the elements of encouragement. They are all designed to help children feel belonging and significance. They are designed to create a sense of capability through the development of life skills such as listening skills and problem-solving skills, and they instill a sense of social interest through the encouragement of helping others.

7

Caring for the Child with Special Needs

Jamie is six years old. Her single mother, Michelle, works long hours and was relieved and grateful to discover Martha's in-home childcare center. When she first called Martha to inquire about childcare, Michelle explained that Jamie has a metabolic disorder called phenylketonuria, *sometimes known as PKU, and has to follow a special diet. "Don't worry," she told Martha, "Jamie knows what she can eat and what she can't, and I usually pack her lunches. She'll be fine."*

But Jamie, like most young children, wants to feel a sense of belonging and wants to be just the same as the other children. When they get special snacks and treats, she wants to eat them, too. Sometimes she trades food from her sack lunch with the other children, giving them the items she's tired of or doesn't like and luxuriating in forbidden foods, away from her mother's nagging and lecturing. Martha doesn't really understand how Jamie's diet is supposed to work, nor does she know the serious consequences of failing to follow it, so she trusts that the little girl is taking care of herself. Martha, unfortunately, is wrong. Jamie is too young to take responsibility for her own health, and her exhausted mother sometimes fails to make sure she has followed her diet.

One afternoon a worker from the local department of social services appears at Martha's door, inquiring about Jamie. Her blood tests have shown disturbing results—not the first time this has happened—and a report of medical neglect has been filed. The worker wants to know whether Jamie has been following her PKU diet. Martha is both alarmed and confused. "I guess so," she tells the worker. "Her mom didn't really explain it to me. I just assumed she was okay." Not long afterward, Jamie leaves Martha's childcare center. She has been placed in a medical foster home, Martha learns later, until her blood levels have stabilized. Martha can only wish she'd understood Jamie's condition well enough to help her.

When we think of children, we usually imagine little boys and girls running, laughing, singing, and jumping. Sometimes we think of children who misbehave, throw toys, and generally complicate our lives and wonder how to deal with misbehavior, discouragement, defiance, or other developmental issues. But for some children, life is far more complicated. They do not see, hear, or perceive their world as other children do, or their bodies function only with the aid of medications or special diets. Some must use wheelchairs or need braces to walk; some have no control of their bladders or bowels, even though they are much older than the normal age for toilet training.

These children, too, appear in childcare centers. Sometimes they have already been diagnosed, and their parents are looking for caregivers who can support and manage their child's disability. Sometimes, too, a child just behaves differently from the others, and teachers struggle to understand why. Children arrive in childcare centers with fetal alcohol syndrome, asthma, diabetes, attention deficit disorder, metabolic disorders, autism, sensory integration dysfunction, developmental delays, and a host of other problems. In fact, many of these diagnoses are increasing among children, for reasons that no one fully understands.

Childcare providers usually aren't doctors; they aren't trained in medical diagnosis or treatment. Yet it is highly likely that you will encounter special needs children at some point in your childcare career. How can you best help these children and their parents, as well as the other children you must care for? What do childcare providers need to know about recognizing and caring for children with special needs?

The Americans with Disabilities Act

ALL PARENTS WORRY about finding the "right" childcare environment for their child. For parents of children with special needs, this issue is even more critical. In 1992, the Americans with Disabilities Act (ADA) became law and expanded the resources available to children with special needs. The ADA states that children with disabilities are entitled to participate in *any* childcare setting (including private or in-home centers) that is available to children without disabilities. The only exception to this requirement is if a child's pres-ence poses a direct threat to the health or safety of others. All childcare centers (except those run by religious organizations), regardless of their size or number of staff, must comply with the require-ments of the ADA.

Childcare centers and providers are required to create a safe and comfortable setting for children with disabilities and special needs. They may, for in-stance, be required to modify their policies and pro-cedures, remove structural barriers, or provide aids and services such as interpreters to allow communi-cation with children who have hearing, speech, or vision impairments. Centers must also train staff

> The ADA states that children with dis-abilities are entitled to participate in any childcare setting (in-cluding private or in-home centers) that is available to children without disabilities.

appropriately and adapt curriculum if necessary. They must dispense medica-tion to children who require it and provide diapering services to children who need it (regardless of their age) if they also diaper younger children. They can-not pass the cost of these services on to the families of special needs children.

Parents whose children are turned down by a childcare facility can file a com-plaint with the United States Department of Justice, and violation of the ADA can result in investigation and even fines. For more information on the ADA and how it may affect your childcare center, you can visit the Department of Justice's Web site at www.usdoj.gov/crt/ada/adahom1.htm, or call the information line at (800) 514-0301. Information is also available at Special Child (www.special-child.com) and the Child Care Law Center (www.childcarelaw.org).

Partnership with Parents

IT IS ALWAYS important that parents and caregivers communicate clearly and often, that they take time to check in with each other, and that they have a way to solve problems when they arise. But for parents and caregivers of special needs children, communication and problem solving are especially critical.

Remember Jamie, the child with PKU whose story began this chapter? Jamie's health was compromised in part because her mother and her childcare provider failed to truly work together to maintain her medical diet. Michelle didn't explain Jamie's condition clearly to Martha and didn't give her a dietary list to follow; Martha didn't ask for more information and assumed that everything was fine. If Martha had known that PKU can result in brain damage or even death, she might have been motivated to learn more and to monitor Jamie's snacks and lunches more closely.

> For parents and caregivers of special needs children, communication and problem solving are especially critical.

But no caregiver can know everything. If a parent brings a special needs child to you for care, you can ask some questions and follow certain procedures that will help you, the parents, and the child get along well together and maintain that child's health and safety. Here are some suggestions:

- **Ask lots of questions, and arrange to exchange information regularly.** Childcare providers and preschool teachers sometimes fear they will be too intrusive if they ask detailed questions about a child's condition and treatment. But as we learned with Jamie, too little information can be dangerous. It is wise to sit down with a child's parents and to learn about the specific diagnosis, the consequences of the illness or condition, and the treatment or care that may be required from you. As much as possible, get this information in writing, and share it with any teachers or caregivers who may work with that child. Information will also help you know when a child's behavior requires intervention from you and when it is directly related to an illness or disability. Special needs children sometimes misbehave, just like all children, because they are two, or three, or six; at other times, their behavior is a result of their special circumstances. Information and understanding will help you know how to respond.

- **Gather information from all available sources and keep written records.** You may want to ask permission from the parents to speak directly to a child's pediatrician, nutritionist, therapist, or other medical team members to learn all you can. Some caregivers find it helpful to keep a daily care notebook in a child's backpack. Details of the child's care, medication, and behavior and any problems or special circumstances that were encountered can be noted each day for parents, who can then write similar instructions or observations about the time a child spends at home. Arranging for weekly check-in conversations will also be helpful; be sure to involve all staff members who have worked with the child that week. If diet or medication is involved in the child's care, be sure to keep written records.

> It is wise to sit down with a child's parents and to learn about the specific diagnosis, the consequences of the illness or condition, and the treatment or care that may be required from you.

- **Keep your observations simple, specific, and positive.** Parents will find it much easier to listen and respond to any problems you are having if you make an effort to give them information about their child that is concrete and nonjudgmental. For instance, instead of telling a concerned mother, "Marty was a behavior problem again today," you might say, "Marty did a lot of throwing today and had a hard time sitting still." Let parents know how you responded and what results you received. Don't hesitate to ask for parents' suggestions in dealing with new or difficult behavior.

- **Invite parents to visit.** It will help both you and the parents of a special needs child to feel comfortable when everyone is familiar with the routine of the childcare day and the way the child responds to it. Inviting parents to visit and observe whenever possible will help all of you work and communicate together.

- **Check with parents about the level of self-care a child is capable of.** In many cases, children are encouraged to assume responsibility for some aspects of their own care as they grow older. Children with metabolic disorders, for instance, are encouraged to measure their own formula and keep track of foods. Older children and teenagers with diabetes can begin to test their blood sugar, count carbohydrates, and administer insulin shots (or maintain their own insulin pump, if that is their method of treatment). Asthmatics usually carry their own inhalers and can learn when they should be used. It is essential that you understand clearly what the child's responsibilities might be and what you must supervise. Get specific instructions, in writing if possible, from parents, and be sure all of the child's teachers understand them. Avoid providing special service, treating the child with excessive sympathy, or doing things for the child that he could do for himself. All children deserve the right to grow to their fullest potential, and doing too much for a child (or making him feel unnecessarily "different") can damage his self-esteem.

> Avoid providing special service, treating the child with excessive sympathy, or doing things for the child that he could do for himself.

- **Be sensitive to the needs and feelings of parents.** Parents of a special needs child are often struggling to accept their child's differences. Sometimes they feel guilt, depression, or a sense of responsibility for the difficulties their child faces. Money is often in short supply, as is time, and siblings frequently resent the time, therapies, and special treatment a special needs child requires. In some cases, in which a child's illness is so severe as to threaten both quality and length of life, grief may be a constant companion for parents—and for caregivers. Be patient, remember to take good care of yourself, and try not to take the occasional tense or difficult days personally. You are providing an invaluable service for the family of a special needs child.

Children with special needs benefit greatly from the opportunity to spend time with other children, to learn, to grow, and to enjoy as much of life as they can. The other children in your childcare center will benefit, too: They have the opportunity to learn compassion, generosity, and kindness; to make a contribution to someone else's welfare; and to understand that all people are worthy of respect and dignity, regardless of their abilities.

"I'm Concerned About This Child": When to Make a Referral

Diane was exasperated—again. Three-year-old Jack, the newest addition to her classroom, just wouldn't listen to her. When she called the children to come in after their outdoors playtime, he refused to respond until she walked over and gently took his

BUILDING A PARTNERSHIP WITH THE PARENTS OF SPECIAL NEEDS CHILDREN

- Ask lots of questions, and arrange to exchange information regularly.
- Gather information from all available sources and keep written records.
- Keep your observations simple, specific, and positive.
- Invite parents to visit.
- Check with parents about the level of self-care a child is capable of.
- Be sensitive to the needs and feelings of parents.

arm. When she called the children for circle time or asked them to get their mats for quiet time, Jack remained in his own world, steadfastly ignoring every word she said. When she walked over to him, he smiled sweetly at her—but he never cooperated with her requests unless she was standing right in front of him.

One day, as the children were working on their art projects, Diane dropped a tray of paint tins and brushes. All of the children shrieked, laughed, and jumped up—all of them, that is, except Jack, who continued quietly to brush paint on his paper. Suddenly everything she'd been noticing made sense to Diane. She walked over behind Jack and clapped her hands behind him; Jack never stirred. Diane shared her suspicions with her supervisor, who then sat down with Jack's mother for a conversation. Jack's mother had also been curious about his behavior, but Jack was easy-going most of the time and she had assumed that their noisy home (Jack had four older brothers and sisters) made it hard for him to hear her.

Sure enough, a visit to an audiologist confirmed Diane's observations: Jack had a significant hearing loss. He hadn't been ignoring her and refusing to cooperate; he simply couldn't hear her. Treatment and therapy opened up Jack's world, and it wasn't long before he was able to talk—and listen—with the other children.

Childcare providers, early childhood educators, and teachers are in a unique and important position. Because they spend hours with children each day, they have the opportunity to observe children closely and to notice both their strengths and their struggles. Caregivers are often the first to notice that a child needs special help. Sometimes teachers and caregivers find themselves watching a particular child more closely than the others. Something may "feel" wrong or different; your instincts may tell you that a child's reactions or behavior are unusual for her age or abilities. It is essential that you and your staff understand age-appropriate behavior and development, but what should you do if a child seems not to be quite "normal"?

It is important that you become a keen observer of the children in your care; it is also important that you *listen*. Listen to the things parents share when they drop off a child in the morning; listen to their concerns about that child's behavior. Many parents already harbor fears that something is "wrong" with their child; support and encouragement from a concerned caregiver can help reassure them and provide information so that they can get appropriate diagnosis and treatment, if necessary. Listening to children is equally important: Listen both to their words and their behavior. The little girl who tells you that her socks "hurt" her and the little boy who is always "too tired" to sit up straight during circle time or go out to play may be giving you more accurate information than you—or they—could guess.

> Caregivers are often the first to notice that a child needs special help.

What sorts of things should you be aware of? Although a complete guide to understanding the disabilities and conditions that can affect children is well beyond the scope of this book, here are some concepts to keep in mind. (Remember that many of these variations can lie well within the range of "appropriate" development or temperament; only if you observe repeated and excessive instances of these traits should you be concerned.)

- **A child is not responsive to her surroundings or to other people.** As Diane learned with Jack, a child who fails to respond normally to sounds or visual cues may be suffering from vision or hearing problems. Young children especially have no way to compare the way they perceive their world with the way others do, and they cannot tell you that their hearing or vision is a problem.

- **A child is overly sensitive to touch, sound, or movement.** Some children feel everything intensely. Their clothing chafes and hurts them, sounds are loud and irritating, and movement seems to frighten them; they may avoid swinging, climbing, or running altogether.

- **A child is unusually insensitive to touch, sound, or movement.** Some children seem unaware of pain, heat, or the actions of others. They may spin, swing, or rock constantly in an effort to stimulate or sooth themselves, or they may engage in solitary, repetitive play, unwilling to allow anyone else to interact with them.

- **A child is unusually awkward.** All children stumble and trip occasionally, especially when they're working on mastery of new physical skills. But some children trip constantly over their own feet, the furniture, and objects on the floor; some have poor balance and continually misjudge distances, fall often, or are unable to climb stairs or playground equipment.

- **A child is impulsive and unusually slow to learn from consequences and experience.** Remember, all children (especially boys) are impulsive, likely to act before thinking. But some children seem completely incapable of weighing options, thinking something through, or even learning from a situation they have experienced several times; for instance, they may pour juice into a cup until it overflows over and over again.

> No matter what you may suspect, and no matter how sure you may be about a child's condition, it is unwise to "diagnose" a child for parents.

No matter what you may suspect, and no matter how sure you may be about a child's condition, it is unwise to "diagnose" a child for parents. Different combinations of the situations described here can, for example, indicate the presence of sensory integration dysfunction, attention deficit disorder, or even autism. Diagnosis is the responsibility of a professional who is trained at evaluating young children. You may be providing the most important service possible simply by bringing your observations to a parent's attention.[1]

---

1. Several excellent books are available that will help you understand differences in the perceptions and abilities of young children and when you should be concerned. Among them are Carol Stock Kranowitz, *The Out-of-Sync Child: Recognizing and Coping with Sensory Integration Dysfunction* (New York: Perigee, 1998); John Taylor, *Helping Your ADD Child*, 3rd Edition (Roseville, CA: Prima, 2001); Edward M. Hallowell and John J. Ratey, *Driven to Distraction: Recognizing and Coping with Attention Deficit Disorder from Childhood Through Adulthood* (New York: Touchstone, 1994); and Ross W. Greene, *The Explosive Child* (New York: HarperCollins, 2001).

WHEN TO BE CONCERNED: CLUES THAT A CHILD MAY NEED HELP

- A child is not responsive to her surroundings or other people.
- A child is overly sensitive to touch, sound, or movement.
- A child is unusually insensitive to touch, sound, or movement.
- A child is unusually awkward.
- A child is impulsive and unusually slow to learn from consequences and experience.

Making a Referral

WHEN YOU SUSPECT that a child may be having problems well beyond the behavior or social skills issues that are typical of childhood, what should you do? When you are convinced that action is necessary, schedule a time to sit down and speak at length with the child's parent. (Pick-up and drop-off times are not appropriate moments for this sort of conversation, nor should the child be present while you are speaking.) Share your observations calmly and kindly. It is difficult to know how a parent will react; she may not agree with you, may struggle to understand what you are telling her, or may be relieved that someone else has noticed a problem.

Regardless of where you work or what sort of childcare facility you have, it is a good idea to compile a list of local referrals and to keep it handy for parents. (Note that you cannot refer a child to a specialist or program without a parent's permission.) You may be able to learn about programs and resources by talking to other providers and teachers or by contacting your local childcare association. Most states offer diagnosis and evaluation services to children from birth to three years of age through a state special children's clinic; other communities may have programs to evaluate speech, hearing, and vision. You may want to get names of licensed therapists who work with young children in your community as well as pediatric neurologists; occupational, speech, or physical therapists; or other specialists.

It can be stressful and intimidating to talk with parents about a child's problems, but your intervention may make all the difference between a child who struggles to get along and one who can thrive with both adults and peers.

> Regardless of where you work or what sort of childcare facility you have, it is a good idea to compile a list of local referrals and to keep it handy for parents.

Children All Together

It is circle time at the Small Wonders Preschool and Kindergarten. Kim, the kindergarten teacher, smiles at her group, who are all sitting on the bright red carpet—all, that is, except Timmy, who smiles back from his wheelchair. Timmy has cerebral palsy and cannot walk, but he is an important part of the group nonetheless.

"Whose turn is it to be Timmy's buddy today?" Kim asks. "Can one of you check our chart?" Ryan, a freckled redhead, runs to look at the laminated poster board on the wall near Kim's chair. "It's Juanita's turn today," he informs the group. Juanita grins and goes to her place behind Timmy's wheelchair.

The five- and six-year olds are proud of the way they help Timmy and enjoy taking turns helping him with his lunch, pushing his wheelchair outdoors, and sharing toys with him. Kim and the other staff members diaper Timmy and make sure he is safe and comfortable, but they have a dozen eager helpers. Timmy is a part of the class, holding the talking stick during class meetings and sharing time; talking is hard for Timmy and the words come out slowly, but the children wouldn't dream of interrupting him, and they protect him fiercely from anyone who might try to tease him. Timmy is one of them, and everyone is richer because of it.

At the end of the day, when Timmy's dad comes to pick him up, his buddy for the day helps carry his backpack out to the car. Timmy's dad knows all the boys and girls and always thanks them for their help by name; sometimes he brings cupcakes or cookies for the class. The children are learning kindness and the joy that comes from helping someone else. Besides, Timmy has a great smile, and they love to make him laugh.

A special needs child can give other children an opportunity to understand differences, to be sensitive to the needs of others, and to use their power to include and help instead of exclude and hurt. If the special needs child is old enough, you can work together to explain her special circumstances and let the other children help you make a list of how they can help. Prejudice evaporates when children are educated and invited to help.

> Prejudice evaporates when children are educated and invited to help.

The same Positive Discipline tools that work with other children will also help special needs children get along, feel a sense of belonging, and avoid misbehavior. You may need to consider cognitive ability, speech and language skills, or physical limitations when using some of the tools, but you can be assured that special needs children, too, benefit from kind, firm discipline that teaches, as well as an attitude of encouragement and respect. Punishment, shame, humiliation, and scolding are no more effective with special needs children than they are with anyone else.

Having a special needs child in your childcare facility will undoubtedly change your routine; it may create extra work and even extra worry. But you may be surprised at the benefits you and the other children in your care receive. Children, no matter how special or different, are still children; all of them deserve respect, dignity, kindness, and the opportunity to experience belonging and significance.

PART 2

Childcare
Topics A–Z

Anger

Child Development Concept

Most teachers, caregivers, and parents understand that all of us, adults and children, get angry from time to time. At least, they understand the concept intellectually; they may truly believe that they should help children understand and manage their anger in constructive ways. But somehow there's something about an angry child that can make an adult's best intentions disappear. Angry children scream, cry, and throw things; they may hit others, damage property, or bang their heads. Teachers and parents alike find these displays frightening and may feel just as out-of-control as the child.

Mad is one of a child's first feeling words. It is also one of the first feelings children learn is unacceptable to adults. "Don't use that tone of voice with me!" adults say with furrowed foreheads. Or, "Don't get angry with me, young lady!" But anger, like most emotions, doesn't go away on command and even children can have good reason to feel angry sometimes.

Imagine for a moment a cast-iron pot bubbling away on a fire. You can easily see the smoke, but unless you look closer, you will not see the contents of the pot. Anger is like smoke; it is easy to see, but it can blind you to the real problem—whatever is bubbling inside the pot. Children can become

angry because they are hurt, frightened, frustrated, worried, lonely, misunderstood, or treated disrespectfully. Young children, in particular, need help in recognizing and labeling their anger, understanding where it comes from, and learning how to manage it in ways that do not hurt themselves or those around them.

Suggestions

1. When confronted with an angry child, remain calm and kind yourself. This may mean taking a moment to count to ten or take a deep breath, but it will not help a child regain control of his emotions if you lose control of yours.

2. Provide an acceptable way to deal with angry feelings. You cannot work on solutions with a child while she is angry. You may invite her to take a positive time-out in your "feel-good" spot—or go yourself—(page 51), or you may use a class meeting to create an "Anger Wheel of Choice" with acceptable ways of blowing off steam. Choices might include running fast around the playground, hitting a "bop bag," pounding wooden pegs with a hammer, mashing clay, or using puppets to express your feelings. The feel-good spot and the class meeting agenda could also be included on the Anger Wheel of Choice, because the child may feel even more empowered by being able to choose and practice these valuable life skills. Choices that hurt the child or others, whether physically or verbally, or that damage property are not appropriate.

3. When a child has calmed down, you can ask simple questions to learn what happened. Use active listening (page 61) to help discover the true cause of the anger: "It sounds like Jenny hurt your feelings, and you wanted to hurt her back," or "You must have felt frustrated when Matthew grabbed your truck." Validating a child's feelings helps her feel understood and is often enough to defuse the anger. If appropriate, you may work together on solutions to the problem or put it on the agenda for a class meeting.

4. Ask the child what she notices happening in her body when she gets really angry. Because anger triggers a number of physical reactions (heart rate and respiration increase, blood vessels expand, muscles tighten, etc.), most people experience anger physically. If the child reports that she gets a knot in her stomach, her fists clench, or her face feels hot (all common responses), you may be able to help her recognize when she's getting

really angry and provide ways to cool off *before* anger gets out of control.

5. Invite the child to draw a picture of how her anger feels. Where in her body does it live? What color is it?

Does it have a sound? Making feelings real can help children learn to deal with them.

6. If the child has difficulty identifying her feelings, show her the feelings

Feeling Faces Chart

faces on the previous page and ask her whether she can find one that expresses how she feels.

7. Validate a child's feelings—even the unpleasant ones—instead of trying to talk her out of them. Accept that children feel what they feel and work on ways to find solutions, clean up messes, and learn from mistakes. You cannot "fix" children's feelings, even if you try. Even difficult feelings can provide opportunities for teaching and encouragement.

Tips for Working with Parents

Parents, too, struggle to understand and deal with children's anger. You may want to use the suggestions offered here to prepare a handout for parents to use in working with their own children. Give parents a copy of the feeling faces so they can use them to help their children identify and express their feelings at home. When one child in your care is frequently angry or aggressive, it may be wise to schedule a time to speak privately with her parents. Frequent angry behavior often is a signal that something is going on at home, and the family may benefit from counseling or parenting classes. Understanding that a child is coping with divorce, illness, or other family stress can help you manage her behavior more calmly and take it less personally.

Apologize, Children Who Won't

Child Development Concept

During a lecture at the National Association for the Education of Young Children in 2000, Bev Bos[1] said, "Telling a child to say 'I'm sorry' makes as much sense as demanding that a child say 'I'm Italian'—even when she isn't."

Caregivers who have studied child development know that the intellectual capabilities of young children have not developed to the point where they can think like adults (see the

---

1. Bev Bos is the director of the Roseville Community Preschool, owner of Turn the Page Press, and author of *Together We're Better: Establishing Coactive Environments for Young Children.* She is a popular workshop presenter and speaker for Early Childhood Conferences.

sidebar on "Piaget Demonstrations"), yet many adults act as though they should. Forcing a young child to "say you are sorry" is an excellent example.

Suggestions

1. While upset, children do not have access to rational thinking. Don't expect a child to do or say anything until she has had time to calm down.

2. Allow time for cooling off. This may mean comforting the child for a while, validating her feelings, removing her from an upsetting situation (while comforting and/or validating feelings), or simply allowing her to spend some time in a positive time-out area (see page 51) until she feels better if this is her choice about what will be most helpful for her. Help the child express her own feelings before helping her consider someone else's feelings. Point to the feelings faces chart (page 135) and let her choose a picture that expresses her feelings if she can't verbalize them without help.

3. Use "what" and "how" questions (see page 62) to help the child explore what happened, how she feels about it, and what ideas she has to solve the problem. Part of this process might be to ask, "How do you think the other person feels?" Again, it may be helpful to look at the feelings faces.

4. After the child has calmed down, feels validated for her feelings, and possibly has identified the other person's feelings, she might be guided to apologize—only if it is her idea. This sometimes happens by asking, "What would make you feel better? Would it help you if the other person gave you a hug or said she was sorry?" Once the child has identified what might make her feel better, you could ask, "Would you be willing to help the other person feel better? What could you do, and when would you like to do it?"

Helping a child decide to do something for someone else (and it may not be an apology) is much different than *demanding* that they do. The point is to help the child think things through in a friendly environment (which invites sincere concern) instead of demanding an apology (which often invites rebellion or just plain confusion).

5. If the child still doesn't feel like doing anything for the other person, express your faith that she will soon learn to care about and help others.

Tips for Working with Parents

Parents often demand that their children apologize because they are

PIAGET DEMONSTRATIONS

Jean Piaget was one of the pioneers in understanding the cognitive development of children. He devised these demonstrations to help adults understand how children's thinking differs from their own:

- Take two balls of clay that are the same size. Ask a three-year-old whether they are the same. Make adjustments by taking clay from one ball and adding it to the other until the child agrees that they are the same size. Then, right in front of her, smash one ball of clay. Then ask her whether they are still the same. She will say no and will tell you which one she thinks is bigger. A five-year-old will tell you they are the same and can tell you why.

- Find four glasses: two glasses that are of the same size, one glass that is taller and thinner, and one glass that is shorter and fatter. Fill the two glasses that are the same size with water until a three-year-old agrees they are the same. Then, right in front of her, pour the water from one of these glasses into the short, fat glass and the other one into the tall, thin glass. Then ask her whether they still hold the same amount of water. Again, she will say no and will tell you which glass she thinks contains the most water. A five-year-old will tell you they contain the same amount and can tell you why.

Both of these examples demonstrate thinking abilities identified by Piaget. When we understand that perceiving, interpreting, and comprehending an event are so markedly different for young children, our expectations as adults alter. The meaning children attach to their experiences does not match the meaning adults attach to the same experiences.

embarrassed by their behavior. Help parents understand that you are more interested in long-term, sincere results than in short-term insincerity. You also have an opportunity to educate them about intellectual development so they can understand that children don't think like adults. The demonstration presented in the sidebar may help.

Biting

Child Development Concept

If biting was a phase that all children went through, it would be easier for caregivers and parents to grit their own teeth and wait for it to pass. However, only a few children provide this challenge—which includes the challenge to remember that children are wonderfully unique. Most children under the age of three do not have the language or social skills to get their needs met in respectful ways. Biters are not "bad" children. They are children who have developed their own unique way to deal with frustration.

Suggestions

1. Supervise, supervise, supervise. We know you were hoping for something else, but one of the authors spent an entire afternoon in a university library researching the subject of biting in early childhood journals. The accumulated wisdom of the researchers amounted to this: If you know a child bites, you must supervise him carefully.

2. If you know a child is a biter, notice the kinds of situations that create frustration and do your best to remove the child from the situation before he takes a chunk out of another child's anatomy.

3. Do not punish. Do not bite back. Remember that children learn what they live. Be an example of respectful behavior.

4. If your careful supervision is too late (after all, you don't have eyes in the back of your head), comfort both the bitee and the biter. Do not make the biter the "bad guy." You have two arms. Take both children on your lap or kneel with an arm around each child. After the crying stops (and it will if you don't add fuel to the flames with punishment), you might let the biter help you put some antiseptic or an ice cube on the bitee.

5. Validate the feelings of the biter: "You wanted the toy, and you feel upset."

6. Gently teach children to "Use your words. Next time you want a toy, ask for a turn." Of course, the child likely won't understand what you are saying, but keep teaching until the child is developmentally ready to absorb the lesson. Patience and the willingness to repeat lessons

until they are learned are essential when working with young children.

7. When you know that a child has a tendency to bite, you can keep something to bite on, such as a clean wash cloth, handy.

Tips for Working with Parents

Which is worse—to be the parent of the biter or the parent of the bitee? This is a toss-up. The parent of the bitee is usually angry and wants "something to be done." The parent of the biter is usually embarrassed and hopes something can be done. Something can be done (as seen in the prior suggestions), but it is not the magic pill both parents may hope for.

Let parents know that you know how painful this is for both of them *and* that you do not believe that treating a child (the biter) disrespectfully is the way to teach respect. It is also wise to point out that the bitee is unlikely to benefit from being treated as a victim. Let them know what you have learned about child development and that you will do your best to supervise carefully.

If the parent of the bitee is angry and insists that you do something different, patiently explain that your goal is to treat all children respectfully. Yes, a parent who believes in punishment may decide you are not the best person to care for his or her child. On the other hand, remaining calm, kind, and firm will be an excellent model for the parent.

Chores/Jobs

Child Development Concept

Chores or jobs provide an excellent opportunity for children to develop a sense of belonging and significance through helping and contributing. Children also can learn responsibility, self-discipline, life skills, and cooperation. Last, but not least, they can develop the belief that "I am capable."

Does all of this come naturally? Yes and no. Have you noticed that most two-year-olds are eager to help? "Me do it," they plead. Too often they are told, "No, you are too little." It is easy

LUNCH AT TOT TOWN

Tot Town is a childcare center that includes many routines that provide children with the opportunity to experience their capability to help and contribute. Lunchtime is a good example. After the director, Joyce, goes shopping, she backs her station wagon to the gate and calls the children to gather around and help carry the groceries into the kitchen. Each child takes one item at a time. The cook tells them where to put the item when possible or has them set the item on a low table so she can put it away.

Two or three children take turns helping prepare the meal by stirring, pouring, tearing lettuce, or whatever they can do. Other children help set the table. Then food is set on the table in small bowls that can be passed around. Children dish up their own food and pour their own milk from small plastic pitchers. They had first participated in "time for training" that included "what" and "how" questions. "What happens if you take too much and there isn't enough for others?" (Others won't get any.) "What could you do if you take a little and are still hungry after you finish it?" (You can ask for more.)

When the children are finished, they go through the clean-up assembly line. They first scrape their uneaten food into a plastic tub, rinse their dishes in another plastic tub filled with water, and then set their dishes on a tray that goes to the dishwasher. Two children take turns helping to load the dishwasher.

for them to get the message that they can't do it well enough—and shouldn't bother asking. If they hear this message often enough, they will believe it. Soon they develop the habit of having others do things for them, and they learn to like it. Who wouldn't like having slaves to wait on you hand and foot? This is when it becomes a real chore to get kids to *do* chores.

Suggestions

1. Appeal to children's desire to help. Use the words "I need your help."

2. Create job charts. When children are four and older, let them help brainstorm the jobs that need to be done and let them help create job charts that assign specific tasks to specific children. Note: It is helpful to have as many jobs as you have children.

3. Include jobs as part of the daily routine. Singing songs or playing special "job music" might be part of the job routine.

4. When children refuse, ask, "What do you need to be doing now to follow our routine?"

5. Another possibility for reluctant children is to invite them to choose a job-sharing buddy. This increases belonging, and the "buddies" can help each other with their jobs.

6. Use your sense of humor with reluctant children: "Here comes the tickle monster to get children who aren't doing their jobs!" After some silly teasing, try one of the prior suggestions.

Tips for Working with Parents

Let parents know that they, too, engage in master/slave training (when they do too much for their children) or responsibility/cooperation training by following the suggestions outlined here.

Clinginess

(see also *Crying*)

Child Development Concept

As in every behavior, clinginess can happen for many reasons. A very young child may be experiencing separation anxiety, a normal developmental phase during which children seem to believe a person who leaves them has actually disappeared—with the obvious result that children cry, cling, and whimper. Some children cling because they have learned it works to manipulate adults. Many children have been pampered and haven't had the opportunity to learn (through experience) that they are capable of handling many different situations, including separation.

Suggestions

1. When children are first introduced to your childcare environment, invite parents to stay for several hours so children and parents both may become familiar with the setting.

2. After the initial familiarization, when children are brought to your care, ask parents to leave as soon as possible. Many children are fine as soon as their parents leave.

3. Rock the child for a while if possible or invite an older child to rock a younger child.

4. Sometimes it is best to allow the child to work things out himself. In other words, don't coax or pay undue attention. Have faith in the child to feel his feelings and learn that he can handle the situation. Offer reassuring smiles and invitations to join the group once in a while, but don't overdo it. Some children take longer than others to adjust.

Tips for Working with Parents

Many parents don't have enough faith in their children to handle difficult situations. Handling the situation may mean feeling upset or anxious for a while. (After all, worry and disappointment are a part of life, and children will do best when they learn they can handle even difficult feelings—with support and encouragement from caring adults.) When

children are pampered, overprotected, and rescued, they don't have the opportunity to exercise their capability skills. On the other hand, children need to feel secure before they can develop independence. Finding the balance is always a challenge. Your parents might find some inspiration from the following story.

Mellie was always trying to cling to her mom, Mrs. Lorey. Mrs. Lorey kept pushing Mellie away because she wanted her daughter to develop independence. It didn't help. Mellie kept clinging to her mother.

One day Mrs. Lorey attended a local festival with a friend and passed a fortune-teller. She and her friend decided to try having their fortunes told "just for fun." The fortune-teller implied that something drastic might happen to Mrs. Lorey before the year was up. Suddenly this adventure wasn't much fun anymore. Mrs. Lorey took the fortune-teller seriously and was certain she was going to die.

Mrs. Lorey changed her attitude about many things. She quit worrying about her daughter's clinging and started clinging to Mellie. She wanted to enjoy every minute with her daughter and was always trying to get her to sit on her lap. Mellie loved this—for a while. Then she began to feel smothered and often pulled away from her mother, asserting her independence.

The year passed, Mrs. Lorey didn't die, and Mellie became a happy, independent child. Even though it wasn't intentional, it seems that Mrs. Lorey had found the balance of helping Mellie feel secure enough that she was ready to quit clinging.

Cooperate, Children Who Won't

Child Development Concept

Most donkeys won't cooperate until their owners learn what motivates them. Carrots work much better than sticks. Instead of blaming a child for not cooperating, perhaps adults need to learn how to motivate children. We will focus on motivation for the moment, but it is important to remember that the child development issues discussed in other subjects (such as children not being developmentally ready for

CREATE ROUTINE CHARTS
WITH YOUR CHILDREN

Objectives

1. To help parents/teachers learn skills for motivating children to cooperate
2. To create structure and routines for daily tasks that need to be done

Materials

Flip chart; markers

Directions

1. Start by creating a typical bedtime routine.
2. Ask for a volunteer to role-play a three-year-old.
3. Ask the "three-year-old" to think of all the things that need to be done at bedtime. As he or she mentions things that need to be done, write them on the flip chart. The list might include such tasks as picking up toys, putting on pajamas, bathing, brushing teeth, swapping hugs and kisses, and reading a story.
4. Look at the list together and ask what is first, second, third, and so on. For example, "Do you take a bath first or put on your pajamas first? Story before hugs and kisses?" Write the numbers in front of each task showing what comes first, second, and so forth.
5. On another flip chart, make a list of the tasks in order, leaving enough space for pictures.
6. Ask the volunteer to draw a picture of himself doing one of the tasks. (Point out that the child could later draw a picture to represent all of the tasks.) Another possibility is to take Polaroid pictures of the child doing each task or to cut pictures from magazines. (This is a favorite for children—to actually see themselves doing each task.)

(continues)

7. Ask the volunteer where in the house the poster should be posted so it can be seen and followed easily.

8. Point out that charts can be made for morning routines, mealtime routines, after school, and so forth.

Comment

It is very important to let the routine chart become the boss. Instead of telling children what to do, ask them, "What is next on our routine chart?"

some things adults expect of them, frustration due to lack of language capabilities, and frustration due to lack of skills) may also be factors when a child can't or won't cooperate.

Suggestions

1. Remember that children need a sense of autonomy and personal power. This is why choices are so valuable: "Would you like to help clean up in the block area or the housekeeping area? You decide."

2. Children usually like to help when invited to do so instead of being *told* what to do. "I really need your help. Can you see what needs to be done in the block area?" This encourages thinking skills and helps children feel capable—and encour-

ages them to use their autonomy and personal power in useful ways.

3. Take time for training. Show them step-by-step, then do it with them, and then watch while they do it themselves. Encourage effort, not just success. Let's use the example of putting on socks. Show them how to lay the sock on the floor so the heel is on the bottom. Then show them how to scrunch the socks between their thumbs and fingers so their toes will go in easily. Then show them how to pull the socks on the rest of the way. Let them practice until they become skilled. This process can be practiced in many areas such as cleaning up and putting on other articles of clothing.

4. Hold class or group meetings for children from ages three to six so

they learn how to cooperate through brainstorming for solutions that help each other.

5. Let children help create routine charts (see our example) so they feel a sense of autonomy and power while abiding by limits and the safety of order. (The activity on page 53 is written for parents because it is easier for childcare providers and pre-school teachers to adapt the activity to their settings than it is for parents to adapt it to theirs. You can create routine charts for the routines associated with the morning, lunch, quiet time, afternoon, and getting ready to go home.)

6. It is very important to let the routine chart become the boss. Instead of telling children what to do, ask them, "What is next on our routine chart?"

Tips for Working with Parents

Parents will appreciate learning skills to increase cooperation. Share some of these tips with your parents and show them how to create routine charts at home.

Crying

(see also *Clinging*)

Child Development Concept

Crying is a language. In fact, it is the only language infants and very young children possess. Adults would not be so nervous or annoyed when children cry if they accepted this fact. Children cry for too many reasons to elaborate here, but a few of them are physical discomfort, frustration, fear, pain, or an effort to manipulate adults. No matter what the reason, the best way to deal with crying is with an attitude of dignity and respect.

Suggestions

1. It is never a good idea to tell a child to stop crying (never mind that it rarely works). It is even worse to tell a child, "Big girls/boys don't cry." We know adults mean well when they say, "Don't cry," but that is the same as saying, "Don't communicate. It makes me uncomfortable."

2. Use your intuition (and the Mistaken Goals Chart on page 40) to give you clues about why the child is crying. If crying isn't due to one of the basic reasons mentioned previously, it could be that the child doesn't feel belonging and significance and is using one of the "mistaken" goals of behavior. The child may be crying in an attempt to find belonging through undue attention. He may be using "water power" as a misguided way to seek belonging. The child may feel hurt (possibly because he has been de-

CHOOSING THE HUGGING GOOD-BYE

After following all the guidelines to find a good childcare situation for three-year-old Mark (and knowing that the preschool she picked was excellent), Mrs. Nelsen was distressed when Mark cried every morning when she left him there. Parting was very difficult, and Mrs. Nelsen would leave with a heavy heart. However, she noticed that when she came by to pick him up at the end of the day, Mark didn't want to leave. He was having a great time.

Mrs. Nelsen thought, "Hmmmm. What is wrong with this picture?" Then she remembered hearing that children know their parents' "buttons" and how to push them. She had a "working mother guilt button," and Mark was pushing it with great skill.

That evening Mrs. Nelsen said to Mark, "Let's play a pretend game. Let's pretend you are the mommy and I'll be Mark. When you take me to school, I'll cry and tell you I don't want you to go." Mark thought that was great fun. Mrs. Nelsen cried and held on to his legs. He laughed and laughed. Then she said, "Okay, now you pretend you are Mark and I'm the mommy, and you can cry and hang on to me when I take you to school." Of course, Mark already knew how to do this very well, but he had a hard time crying when it was just pretend. He ended up laughing as he held onto Mrs. Nelsen's legs.

throned by a new baby at home or because he feels abandoned) and feels his only option is revenge (which he takes out on whoever is in his path), or perhaps he feels inadequate and just wants to give up. Each of these goals would be handled differently.

Check the Mistaken Goals Chart for specific ideas.

3. If you sense the crying is due to fear or frustration, do your best to offer comfort. If a child is experiencing separation anxiety, it may help to

They were both laughing as Mrs. Nelsen said, "Well, I know you know how to do a crying good-bye, because you have been doing it every morning. Now let's practice giving a hugging good-bye. You be the mommy first and I'll be Mark. Pretend you have just taken me to school." Mark took her by the hand and walked her to the imaginary school. Mrs. Nelsen gave him a hug and said, "Bye, Mommy. See you later." Then it was Mark's turn, and he repeated the scene with a good-bye hug. Then Mrs. Nelsen said, "Now you know how to do both a crying good-bye and a hugging good-bye. Tomorrow you can decide which one you want to do."

The next morning Mrs. Nelsen reminded Mark that he could decide to give her a hugging good-bye or a crying good-bye, adding, "I wonder which one you will choose?" Mrs. Nelsen wasn't surprised when Mark decided to give her a hugging good-bye, even though either choice would have been okay with her. Later she shared with a friend that she thought she knew why he chose the hugging good-bye. First, she had given up her guilt button. She felt very confident that Mark was spending his days in an excellent environment. She said, "I don't know how he knew that I no longer had a guilt button, but I know he knew." Second, she had taken time for training so Mark had the skills for a hugging good-bye as well as a crying good-bye—and he knew it was his choice.

hold her for a while. Every childcare environment should have a rocking chair. Sometimes an older child can help comfort or rock a younger child.

4. If you think the child is frustrated, validate her feelings: "You are feeling angry right now." "You wish you could do what the older kids are doing."

5. Sometimes it is okay to simply allow the child to have his feelings. You might say, "It is okay to cry. I hope you feel better soon."

6. If the child has been involved in creating a positive time-out area (see page 51), you might ask, "Would it help you to go to our 'feel-good place' (or whatever your children have decided to call it) for a while?"

7. If you feel the child is crying in an effort to manipulate you, state what you are willing to do or what needs to be done. "I know you want me to put your shoes on for you, but I have faith in you to do it yourself. I'll come back in a few minutes so you can show me what you have done." Or "I know you don't want to help clean up, and now it is cleanup time."

8. Communicate with parents to stay informed about what might be going on at home that is affecting the child's behavior.

Tips for Working with Parents

Parents will feel differently about crying when they understand it is a language. They will be more effective when they learn to understand (not speak) the language. They can also take time to teach skills that may help the child learn other ways to behave and communicate, as in the example in the sidebar.

Defiance

Child Development Concept

Adults rarely appreciate it when children are defiant. But it is wise to ask *why* a child is acting defiant before trying to deal with the behavior. Could it be that the adult has a part in the problem? Could it be that the adult is behaving in controlling or permissive ways that threaten the child's need for autonomy? Could it be that the child simply lacks the social and verbal skills to assert his power in useful ways and thus resorts to defiance? Is he being influenced by too much TV where characters are violent or disrespectful?

Children need to feel a sense of power. Let's put that another way: All children have personal power and will use it in one way or another. It is the job of the caregiver to help them use their power in useful ways.

Suggestions

1. When they are upset, children do not have access to rational thinking. (You probably have heard this state-

ment before, and you will hear it again.) Don't try to reason with a child until he has had time to calm down. Making demands or using any form of punishment invites rebellion and further defiance.

2. Create an atmosphere in which children feel less need to behave defiantly. In other words, treat them as assets (by getting them respectfully involved) instead of as objects (by making demands) or recipients (by doing too much for them).

3. Class meetings (see page 54) are one way to help children feel respectfully involved. They love brainstorming for solutions, and this process allows them to feel capable and helpful.

4. Ask for help and invite the child to use his thinking skills: "I need your help. What could you do to help clean up?" Children love to feel needed and capable.

5. Offer limited choices. It is often best to start with "I need your help." Then you could add, "Would you like to help clean up in the block area or the dress-up area? You decide." Ending with "You decide" is very important. It increases the child's sense of autonomy and useful power.

6. Let children help create routine charts (see page 53) so they feel a sense of autonomy and power while

"I AM CAPABLE"

Objective

To understand social and emotional development and the importance of helping children develop a sense of autonomy versus doubt and shame.

Comment

Erik Erikson discovered the following stages of emotional and social development. The focus of this activity is the second stage, the development of autonomy versus doubt and shame:

0–1   Trust Versus Mistrust

1–2   Autonomy Versus Doubt and Shame

3–6   Initiative Versus Guilt

Directions

1. Make a list of things (including discipline methods) children experience that might invite them to develop a sense of doubt and shame.

2. Make a list of things children experience that might invite them to develop a sense of autonomy.

3. Look at the first list and circle things you have done because you lacked awareness of the fact that they might lead to a sense of doubt and shame in your child.

4. Look at the second list and circle the things you will do on a regular basis to help your child develop a sense of autonomy—the belief that "I am capable."

5. Notice that your child is less likely to be defiant when she feels capable.

abiding by limits and the safety of order. Then the routine chart becomes the boss. Instead of telling children what to do, ask them, "What is next on our routine chart?"

7. Remember that a misbehaving child is a discouraged child. Punishment increases the discouragement—and the misbehavior. Respectfully involving children is encouraging.

Tips for Working with Parents

Parents often are not aware of their part in creating defiance or the fact that their child may be feeling powerless and thus chooses a negative way of expressing his power. Share some of the tips that have been presented here with your parents, as well as the sidebar activity.

Disrespect

Child Development Concept

Behavior always has a purpose. What might be a child's purpose in behaving disrespectfully? You will find as many possibilities as there are children, but we will look at a few possibilities.

We always stress the importance of getting into the child's world to understand behavior. One way to do that is to look at your own feelings. Yes, *your* feelings will be your first clue to understanding the child's purpose—his *mistaken goal.* (See page 4h0.) Of course, the mistaken goal comes from discouragement. Understanding the goal is one step toward understanding the discouragement. (Remember, too, that children are not consciously aware of their mistaken goals, although you may be able to ask questions to confirm your guesses.)

Does the child feel discouraged because she is being treated disrespectfully? There are many ways that adults treat children disrespectfully, even though that is not their intent. It is disrespectful to do too much for children. It is disrespectful to be too controlling with children. And it is disrespectful (as well as ineffective in the long term) to use any form of punishment on children.

Suggestions

1. Treat children respectfully.

2. Avoid permissiveness, control, and punishment. All of these invite children

to act disrespectfully in many forms. Some may become rebellious, some become revengeful, some become demanding, and so on.

3. Respectfully involve children in finding solutions (rather than assigning blame).

4. With children under the age of three, use distraction and redirection instead of name-calling or punishment.

5. Help children feel belonging and significance by needing their help and by letting them know how much you care.

DISRESPECT INVITES DISRESPECT

Objective

For adults to understand how their behavior might motivate their children's behavior.

Instructions

1. Think of a time when someone treated you disrespectfully.
2. Describe what happened.
3. When reliving that situation, how does it make you feel?
4. What would you like to do? Do you feel like cooperating, like rebelling, like getting even, or like disappearing?
5. Think of the last time you treated your child disrespectfully.
6. Describe what happened.
7. Make a guess about what the child felt.
8. What did the child do? Did the child's behavior fit in one of the following categories: rebelling, getting even, or giving up?
9. If you could "do it over," how could you handle the same situation respectfully?

6. Try a hug. When a child is being disrespectful, say, "I need a hug." (Fortunately it is still considered acceptable to hug young children.) Another possibility is to say, "What would help you feel better right now? A hug, a handshake, or a high five?" This is often enough to interrupt the disrespectful behavior long enough to create a feeling of belonging and encouragement before trying something else.

7. Sometimes doing the unexpected also distracts a child from her misbehavior and discouragement and gives both of you a moment to think things through. The unexpected might be to say, "Do you know I really care about you?" Another unex-pected action might be to say, "Let's see who can make the funniest faces for one minute." Both of you may end up laughing, and then you can focus on problem solving.

Tips for Working with Parents

It may be difficult for parents to hear that children may be acting disrespectful because they are being treated disrespectfully, but they need to understand this. Share the sidebar activity with them to increase their empathy about how they would feel and what they would want to do when treated disrespectfully.

Eat, Children Who Won't

Child Development Concept

Eating is another one of those natural bodily functions (like toileting and sleeping) that adults often turn into a battleground by becoming too concerned and too controlling. Eating is rarely as great a problem in an early childhood education center as it is for parents because childcare providers don't have the emotional investment in a child's nutrition and eating habits that most parents do. Still, a child who refuses to eat lunch or snacks, is picky, or constantly trades food with other children can create problems. Parents, too, can put pressure on caregivers to "make" a child eat. (For information on helping children who must follow special diets, see chapter 7.)

Many research studies have demonstrated that children will eat what they need if they are provided with good choices. The problems occur when children have too many poor choices that inhibit the body's natural craving for nutritious food.

Suggestions

1. Create a routine that includes all stages of eating. Allow children four years old and older to help create these routines. The routine might include things that must be done to prepare for a meal (perhaps preparing both food and the table), time for eating, and cleaning up routines.

2. Allow children to help prepare food whenever possible.

3. If they can't help prepare the food, allow them to set the tables and/or help clean up.

4. Put the food on the table and allow children to help themselves instead of serving for them. Even if lunch is simple sandwiches, they can be put on one large plate where children can help themselves. You can use "what" and "how" questions to work with children who take too much food.

5. Do not use dessert as a bribe for eating nutritious food. It may be appropriate to eliminate desserts so they don't become an issue. Or dessert could be cheese or fruit cut into appealing shapes.

MEALTIME TIPS

1. Do not bring junk foods into the house. Of course children won't eat regular meals when they have filled up on snacks or junk foods.

2. Don't try to "make" your children eat anything, as that will only invite power struggles.

3. Do not give your children undue attention for not eating.

4. Avoid lectures about starving children. Instead of having the effect you want, your children will probably tell you to send the food to them.

5. Do not make special meals for your children. (See the next suggestion.)

6. Teach children how to make their own peanut butter sandwiches or tortillas with cheese. Include them in the planning and preparation of meals. Let them know that in the future they can choose between eating what is on the table and making their own sandwiches or tortillas. Then, without making a fuss, let them choose. If they complain about what is on the table, ask, "What do you need to do about that?"

7. Decide on a beginning time and an ending time for meals. Ten to fifteen minutes is usually plenty of time for young children. At the end of the agreed upon time, clear the table. If children complain that they are still hungry (because they have been dawdling), say, "I'm sure you can make it until our next meal." Children will learn from your actions that mealtime is not a time for manipulation.

8. As with every issue, children are more cooperative when they are respectfully involved. Even toddlers can help wash and tear lettuce, set the table, or help in many other ways.

9. When children reach the age of three to four, let them help plan meals. They are more likely to eat what they have helped plan. They can also help with the shopping and meal preparation.

(continues)

10. Avoid products that contain sugar. Sugar can suppress the body's natural craving for good foods.

11. Provide healthy snacks. It is fine if your children don't eat because they have filled up on cheese, carrot sticks, or other healthy snacks. Who said good food should be eaten only at mealtimes?

12. Plan meals around simple foods that children usually enjoy such as spaghetti, macaroni and cheese, tuna casserole, tacos, hamburgers, mashed potatoes and gravy, Jell-O fruit salad, toasted cheese sandwiches, etc. Most children do not like foods that adults consider "gourmet."

13. Be sure your children get a good multiple vitamin and relax.

Adapted from Jane Nelsen, Lynn Lott, and H. Stephen Glenn, *Positive Discipline A–Z*, rev. ed. (Roseville, CA: Prima, 1999).

6. Do not make an issue of eating. Allow children to eat what they want in ten minutes or so. Then follow your clean-up routine.

Tips for Working with Parents

You may find it helpful to share with parents the fact that families did not experience many eating problems with their children during the Great Depression because there was not enough food to go around. If one person didn't want to eat, that left more for others, who were only too happy to oblige. Parents also may be providing special service for children, making separate meals to satisfy the whims and tastes of different children. This encourages picky eating and power struggles over food.

Parents may not be aware that their efforts to protect and control their children are actually creating the opposite of their intentions. They need to know that they may be creating power struggles over a natural bodily function. Share the sidebar's tips with them.

Exclusion

Child Development Concept

"You can't come to my birthday party" is a chapter title in the book *Positive Discipline for Preschoolers*. This phrase says a great deal about the social development of young children. To adults, children often seem cruel; indeed, they can be very hurtful to other children. However, they don't intend to be cruel—they are simply egocentric and are exploring their sense of belonging, significance, and personal power. It is the adult's job to prevent children from hurting other children's feelings as much as possible and to teach them empathy and manners.

Children have different temperaments. Some are more dominant than others. Less dominant children seem to gravitate to the dominant child and almost grovel for her favor. The dominant child recognizes her own power and almost haughtily chooses one child and deliberately excludes another. The "chosen" child has now risen to a powerful position and will diligently fight to keep her place by working as a "team" with the dominant child to exclude other children. These alliances (particularly among girls, who tend to use words as weapons) can change from day to day or

even from hour to hour. (For more information about social skills, see chapter 5.)

Suggestions

1. Take the dominant child aside and teach him to use his power in useful ways. Don't do this during a conflict, but wait until a calm time. You might say, "You are a very good leader and a powerful person. Would you like to use your power to help others or to hurt others?" Most children don't purposely try to hurt others, but they like the feeling of power. When they become aware of their power to hurt or to help, they will usually choose to help.

2. Children don't usually exclude others until they are at least four years old. At this age they are old enough to participate in class or group meetings (see page 54). During a meeting, discuss how it feels when someone is mean to you or won't let you play with them. (It is usually best to avoid talking about specific children.) Allow each child to take turns sharing how this feels. Use the feeling faces on page 135 if he needs help identifying his feelings.

3. After discussing how exclusion feels, invite the children to brainstorm

DO'S AND DON'TS FOR
SUCCESSFUL FAMILY MEETINGS

Do:

1. Remember the long-range purpose: To develop perceptions of belonging, significance, and capability and to teach valuable life skills such as communication skills, problem-solving skills, thinking skills, accountability, and cooperation.

2. Post an agenda in a visible place and encourage family members to write problems—or anything that needs to be discussed by the family—on it as they occur.

3. Start with compliments so family members learn to look for and to verbalize positive things about each other.

4. Brainstorm for solutions to problems. Start with wild and crazy ideas (for fun) and end with practical ideas that are useful and respectful to all concerned. Then choose one suggestion (by consensus) and try it for a week.

for solutions to the problem—what they could do to help others instead of hurt them. Write every idea on a flip chart and post it on a wall where everyone can see it.

4. When you see exclusion taking place, intervene by asking, "Who can remember what we talked about during our group meeting about how it feels when others are mean to you or won't play with you?" Wait until someone remembers and shares at least one idea. Then ask whether anyone remembers anything else. (It is important to *ask* them instead of *telling* them.) Then point to the list of solutions and ask whether anyone can remember some of the solutions to this problem that they decided on. Again, wait for someone to remember. If they can't, ask whether anyone can read the ideas (you may have children old enough to read) or

5. Calendar a family fun activity for later in the week as well as all sports and other activities (including a chauffeur schedule).

6. Keep family meetings short, ten to thirty minutes, depending on the ages of your children. End with a family fun activity, game, or dessert.

Don't:

1. Use family meetings as a platform for lectures and parental control.

2. Allow children to dominate and control. (Mutual respect is the key.)

3. Skip weekly family meetings. (They should be the most important date on your calendar.)

4. Forget that mistakes are wonderful opportunities to learn.

5. Forget that a family meeting is a process that teaches valuable life skills, not an exercise in perfection. Learning the skills takes time. Even solutions that don't work provide an opportunity to go back to the drawing board and try again, always focusing on respect and solutions.

6. Expect children under the age of four to participate in the process. (If younger children are too distracting, wait until they are in bed.)

whether they would like you to read them.

5. Ask the children which of the solutions they would like to try.

6. You might make a Wheel of Choice (see page 164) from the solution list they created or create your own. The list might include such things as take turns playing with each other, say nice things about everyone, make the game bigger so everyone can play, go to another game or area, tell the person how you feel, put the problem on the class meeting agenda, or take turns being the leader. Let the children who are having a problem look at the Wheel of Choice and choose a solution that might help them. Or ask whether they would like to spin the spinner on the Wheel of Choice and follow the solution it points to.

Tips for Working with Parents

Parents need to understand that children don't mean to be cruel but like to feel powerful. For this reason, children need training in how to use their power in useful ways. Share the Wheel of Choice with parents, as well as the sidebar's tips on holding family meetings.

Fighting (over Toys)

Child Development Concept

Children fight for many reasons, but in a childcare situation, it is often over toys. Children under the age of six may fight over a toy because they are very egocentric; they want what they want, and they want it *now*. Have you ever noticed how a certain toy may not be popular until a child picks it up and starts to play with it? Then another child goes for it with the persistence of a crab that won't let go.

Children under the age of three don't have the verbal or social skills to ask for what they want and to consider the feelings of others. Three- to five-year-olds are developing verbal skills, but they use them to make demands rather than to express patience, consideration, and problem-solving skills.

Children who fight are not "bad." They are behaving age appropriately. This does not mean fighting should be ignored in childcare or preschool settings (although this may be one possibility for parents). Children need your supervision and kind and firm guidance to resolve the present problem and to teach them verbal and social skills (which may not take hold until they are long gone from your care). Just know that you are planting seeds that will someday bloom and make the world a more peaceful place.

Suggestions

1. While upset, children do not have access to rational thinking. (Have you noticed that we keep repeating this?)

2. Don't waste time trying to reason with children while they are upset. If a toy is involved, you may need to take it away and put it on a high shelf for a while. However, do not say insulting or silly things such as, "If you two can't share, you can just do without," while doing this. Be kind and firm: "I'll put the toy up for now." Do not take sides, try to play referee, or say, "He had it first." Surely you have noticed this approach doesn't make any difference to squabbling children. That would require reasoning skills that these children don't yet possess.

3. Of course children are going to cry. Comfort as best you can or simply allow them to have their feelings.

4. If possible, enlist the help of older children to help comfort or distract the arguing children. This may take some discussion and advance training during a class or group meeting (see page 54). Let the children brainstorm what they could do to comfort or distract a child who is feeling upset. Help them make a poster of their list and hang it in a visible place for future reference. They will have fun drawing pictures on the poster to remind them of what their suggestions might look like. We hope you are seeing the peacemaking skills you will be teaching older children and the modeling they will be doing for the younger children.

5. Have a timer available. Ask which child would like to set the timer while the other child plays with the toy. This is a distraction that may work. If not, try one of the other suggestions. If it does work, help them (don't automatically do it for them) set the timer to five minutes. (Most children can't wait patiently for longer than that.) At the end of five minutes, the person with the toy trades for the timer. They can keep doing this until one or both loses interest.

6. Take time for training regarding the timer. As soon as children are verbal, show them the timer and how to set it. You might color the five with a bright marker. Let them practice setting the timer to five minutes. Then let them role-play taking turns with a toy and with the timer.

7. Ask children over the age of four whether one of them would be willing to put the problem on the class or

group meeting agenda or whether they would like you to. That will serve as a cooling-off time because they know they will get help later. Children feel very empowered when they know they will be able to use their thinking skills and brainstorming skills to work on solutions.

8. Create a Wheel of Choice. (See the sidebar's activity.)

Tips for Working with Parents

It may be wise to ask parents to be sure that children do not bring toys

WHEEL OF CHOICE

Objective

To provide children with another alternative for problem solving.

Comment

Children feel empowered when they are included in the problem-solving process instead of merely "objects" of the process.

or video games from home, as these are often the items children fight over. Parents need help and encouragement over and over regarding child development and age appropriateness. They also need to be reminded occasionally about your philosophy of kind and firm intervention and modeling for long-term skill building.

Share the Wheel of Choice activity with parents so they can make one at home with their children. Remind them that you focus on solutions whenever possible instead of blame or punishment.

Activity

1. Use the Wheel of Choice as a sample to show your children during a family or class meeting.

2. Draw (or ask a child to draw) a large circle and divide it into pies.

3. Together, decide on one or two typical problems such as fighting or not taking turns. Write them down.

4. Brainstorm some possible solutions to these problems; once you have all agreed on several that would be respectful and helpful, write these solutions in the pie spaces. Leave enough room at the end for symbols or pictures.

5. Draw symbols or pictures to represent each solution.

6. If possible, have the finished wheel laminated and place it where it can be easily seen or found.

7. When children have a problem, invite them to see if they can find a solution on the Wheel of Choice that would work for them.

The Wheel of Choice works best when it isn't the only possibility. It may be more effective to ask children, "Would you like to use the Wheel of Choice, take some positive time-out (or whatever you have named it), or put this problem on the agenda so we can find a solution later?"

Lines

Child Development Concept

Lining up, that staple of life in preschools, childcare centers, and elementary schools, creates all kinds of problems. There's just something about having to stand in line that seems to induce the nicest kids to hit, shove, complain, call names, cut in line, and generally fight the system.

We have often wondered why schools keep insisting on a method that creates more problems than it solves. We are further amazed to see preschool teachers trying to get small children to "line up." Many things are expected of children before they are developmentally ready, and lining up fits in this category. It is an invitation for failure, rebellion, and confusion because young children in particular cannot understand the purpose.

Suggestions

1. We think the reason teachers try to get children to line up is to create order. Because the opposite is often the result, it makes sense to try something else to create order and efficiency.

2. As long as the children can get to and from destinations quickly, quietly, and safely, stop requiring lines. If they have problems, engage them in solving the problems.

3. Of course, our favorite method for solving problems is to involve children (four and older) in class meetings to brainstorm for solutions so they will have ownership in the plans they create. (If they are too young to engage in brainstorming, they are too young to understand lines.) Start by asking for their ideas about how to get from one place to another quickly, quietly, and safely. They might come up with such ideas (with a little prompting) as keep your hands to yourself, know where you are going, and be respectful of those around you.

4. When you have established routines, lines are not necessary. Allow children to move freely from play time to story time to outside time to bathroom time to lunch (or whatever your daily routine includes). If you find a stray child, invite him to look at the routine chart to see what is next.

5. Younger children may need help. Simply take them by the hand (or invite an older child to do so) and lead them to where they need to go next.

6. Lines can help adults keep track of children on field trips. Get a long, thin rope and invite children to line up and hold on to the rope while you are walking any distance such as to a park.

Tips for Working with Parents

Emphasize the importance of having faith in children to be respectful when adults provide them with routines and engage them in problem solving. Parents are more concerned that their children are happy, safe, and respected than that they be able to form a line.

Listen, Children Who Won't

Child Development Concept

Adults train children not to listen. Sorry, but this is another case where adults need to look at their own behavior. Lecturing is a great way to train children not to listen. Too often adults tell, tell, tell (lecture, lecture, lecture). They tell children what happened, what caused it to happen, how they should feel about it, and what they should do about it. This is a very threatening experience for children, and they learn to take care of themselves by shutting down. How do you feel when someone lectures to you? Our guess is that you feel inadequate, bored, irritated, defensive, or downright rebellious. Why would children feel any different?

Suggestions

1. Remember that children will listen to you *after* they feel listened to. So the first thing you can do to train children to listen is to *model* listening.

2. Use reflective listening or active listening. *Reflective listening* is when you reflect back what you heard (without sounding like a parrot): "You don't want to take a nap." "You are angry because she hit you." *Active listening* is when you read between the lines and make some guesses about what the child is feeling—and then check it out to see whether you are correct: "You hit Julie because it made you mad when she took your toy."

3. Validate feelings. Both reflective and active listening are ways of validating feelings. You can also simply say, "I understand. I think I would feel that way, too."

4. Once children feel listened to, they are more willing to listen to you. Then you can throw in a minilecture—*if* it is followed by getting the child involved in problem solving: "I understand that you are angry, and what you feel is always okay. However, what you *do* is another matter. It is okay to feel angry, but it is not okay to hit others. How could you express your anger without hitting?"

5. Brainstorm options *with* children. If they have a hard time getting started, it is okay for you to start the brainstorming: "How about using your words? How about putting the problem on the class meeting agenda

STRATEGIES THAT ENCOURAGE LISTENING

1. Children can learn to be part of a family in which people treat each other with respect when parents give up control and teach cooperation.

2. Model listening. Children listen to you *after* they feel listened to.

3. Have regular family meetings during which all members, including parents, listen to each other and focus on solutions instead of blame.

4. Be respectful when you make requests. Don't expect children to do something "right now" when you are interrupting something they are doing. Ask, "Would you like to take a break and do this now or in twenty minutes? You decide." Adding "You decide" is very empowering. If they choose twenty minutes, ask, "Would you like to set the timer, or do you want me to?"

   Ask your children whether they would be willing to listen to some important information. This statement usually arouses curiosity, and they feel respected because they have a choice. If they agree to listen, they usually will. Otherwise, you might as well skip the lecture, which will fall on deaf ears.

to get some help from others? How about asking Julie if she would use the Wheel of Choice (see page 164) with you to find a solution."

6. Instead of telling, ask "what" and "how" questions. Remember that education is derived from the Latin word *educare,* which means to "draw forth." Lectures are an attempt to "stuff in."

7. Lectures are especially ineffective with children younger than the age of four. They are not developmentally able to absorb and understand lectures the way adults think they can, yet they can be left with a feeling of doubt and shame (discouragement then can lead to misbehavior). The following suggestions are best for children younger than four.

8. When you must give directions, use fewer words—one word is best: "Nap time"; "Clean-up time."

9. Use nonverbal signals: Point at what needs to be done. Smile, but don't say a word.

10. Use action. Take the child by the hand and lead him, kindly and firmly, to the task that needs to be done.

11. When you have created routine charts with children, you can ask them what is next instead of telling them.

12. Children listen carefully when you whisper because they have to listen to hear you. Try it.

Tips for Working with Parents

Parents will benefit from the prior suggestions as well as the ones in the sidebar.

Loud Talking

Child Development Concept

Alfred Adler often said, "Anything can be something else." Loud talking could be seen as disrespectful, or it could be seen as enthusiasm. In either case, it can be a problem that needs to be addressed. Seeing noise as enthusiasm, however, instead of disrespect creates a totally different attitude for dealing with the problem.

Suggestions

1. Let the kids know that loud talking is a problem for you and why it is a problem. Then ask for their help in solving the problem. A class meeting is a good time for brainstorming for solutions.

2. As in many problems, loud talking may need to be solved over and over, especially when it is difficult to curb enthusiasm. Sometimes it works to say, "What did we decide to do about loud talking?" That may be enough of a reminder. Incidentally, it is unrealistic to think that children should never need reminding. Respectful reminding takes less time and is more pleasant than scolding or punishing.

3. Instead of telling the kids when it is appropriate to use loud voices and when it is appropriate to use soft voices, ask them. Remember the magic of involvement. They will come up with the same answers: outside and inside. If they don't, you can use some leading questions such as, "What kind of voices are appropriate inside?" They will still be telling you instead of being told.

4. Another little trick is to ask them to create a signal for a reminder to use softer voices. It might be a tug on the ear, tapping your head, or a peace sign. Let the kids decide. Then when kids are talking loudly during a time they have agreed not to, either give the sign or ask who can remember the signal for soft talking.

Tips for Working with Parents

Let the children share with their parents what they have decided about

where it is appropriate to use loud and soft voices —and their signal for reminding each other. Children feel proud when they can share their skills at problem solving and signals for cooperation.

Lying

Child Development Concept

The topic of lying can teach us so much about child development— and about adults. Most adults lie from time to time, yet they become terribly upset when children lie. That is something to contemplate.

Too many adults do not understand child development and brain development, really believing that children think the way adults do. They do not. What adults call lying may be wishful, imaginary, or magical thinking to young children.

As children become older and actually do lie, the first thing adults should look at is the "why," the belief behind the behavior. Are they lying to protect their sense of autonomy? Are they lying to avoid punishment? Are they lying to avoid embarrassment? Are they trying to protect their privacy or a friend? Are they trying to make themselves look better so they will feel more belonging and significance? (In some ways, children *do* think like adults. These reasons sound like the same reasons adults might lie.) Or, are they simply at the developmental stage where it is not an issue?

Suggestions

1. Understand the basic needs of children to feel belonging and significance, to experience a sense of autonomy (personal power), and to avoid blame, shame, and pain (punishment).

2. Create an environment in which children feel belonging and significance because they are needed and can practice their capability skills and in which they can use their personal power to help and contribute.

3. Create an environment in which it is safe to tell the truth. Be sure you notice when children are truthful, and thank them if appropriate.

4. Help children understand that mistakes are opportunities to learn and that when they make mistakes your focus will be on finding solutions instead of blame or punishment.

5. Do not ask "set-up" questions that invite lying. A set-up question is one for which you already know the answer, such as, "Did you break the toy?" or "Did you wash your hands?" Instead, say something like, "I see that the toy is broken. Do you think it can be fixed, or do you need to throw it away?" "I notice that you didn't wash your hands. What do you need to do before lunch?"

6. If the lie does not involve a mistake or fear of punishment, you might say, "That sounds like a good story. You have such a good imagination. Would you like to draw a picture about that—or several pictures for a storybook?"

7. Be honest and matter-of-fact: "That does not sound like the truth to me. I wonder if you are scared that you might be punished if you tell the truth." This might be followed with "We don't believe in punishment. We know people make mistakes, and we focus on solutions."

8. Take a moment to consider whether the child might be experiencing excessive control from others, perhaps at home or by you. Then find ways to involve the child in shared control (e.g., offering choices or problem solving) so he doesn't have to lie to protect his sense of personal power.

9. Sometimes you can ignore the lie and redirect the child to a solution.

A WORD FROM THE WISE

A mother brought her young child to Ghandi and requested that he tell her child to stop eating sugar because it was bad for him. Ghandi asked the woman to return in three days. When she returned with the child in three days, Ghandi said to the child, "Stop eating sugar. It isn't good for you."

The mother asked, "Why didn't you tell him that three days ago? Why did you make me go away and come back?"

Ghandi said, "I had to stop eating sugar myself before I could tell him to stop."

For example, if a child says, "I didn't break the toy," even though you watched him do it, reply, "I see a broken toy. It doesn't matter who did it. However, I'll bet we can figure out what to do about the toy—and maybe how to prevent toys from getting broken in the future. What are your ideas?" Another possibility would be to say, "I see a broken toy. Would you like to put this problem on our class meeting agenda so we can figure out what to do about it and some ideas to help protect our toys?"

Tips for Working with Parents

Point out the importance of modeling (see the story in the sidebar) and the importance of focusing on solutions instead of blame. You can also help parents understand that there is always a belief behind behavior; children do have reasons for their lies (when they are old enough to lie), and understanding those reasons may give parents clues to resolving the problem.

Mind, Children Who Won't

Child Development Concept

We don't know a single caregiver who enjoys it when a child responds to a simple request with "No!" or "Won't!" But when they discuss behavior, adults usually describe what children do but not what the adult does. Children don't misbehave in a vacuum. Adults often invite power struggles. This does not mean that adults are always responsible for misbehavior. There are many other reasons why children misbehave or refuse to mind, such as mistaken goal behavior (see page 40), divorce, a new baby, or being hungry or tired.

It is also important to understand the child development concept of individuation—the ongoing process in which children explore who they are separate from adults. How will children discover who they are without testing boundaries and exploring their personal power?

Adults need to understand child development and age appropriateness so they know what they can do to encourage and motivate children as well as what they do that is discouraging to children. Children do need to learn cooperation and respect, but they will learn those qualities best when they see them practiced daily by their caregivers, teachers, and parents.

Suggestions

1. Whatever interaction you choose, be sure it is based on kindness and firmness at the same time.

2. The best method for encouraging children under the age of three to mind is kind and firm distraction and redirection.

3. Avoid *telling* older children what to do as much as possible. Instead *ask* them what needs to be done now, what is next on the routine chart, or what ideas they have to help solve the problem. It is easier just to tell, but telling invites resistance. (Remember, the word *educate* comes from the Latin root *educare*, which means "to draw forth," not "to stuff in.") How

well would you mind if you were always being told what to do? Asking invites a child to use his thinking skills and to decide for himself—which is much more motivating.

4. When it is necessary to tell, try using one word or very few words, such as, "Jacket." However, even this could be avoided by asking, "What do you need so you won't be cold outside?"

5. Here it is again: Involve children in brainstorming and problem solving so they are motivated to follow their own solutions and plans.

6. Sometimes it is most effective to shut your mouth and act. Gently take a child by the hand and lead her to what needs to be done.

7. Use the phrase "As soon as . . .": "I'll drive the van as soon as everyone is buckled up." "I (and my helpers) will put lunch on the table as soon as the toys are cleaned up and hands are washed."

8. Decide what *you* will do instead of what the child must do. "I'm not willing to discuss this while we are both upset. I will get back to you as soon as I have calmed down." What a great example for children when you can take responsibility for your own

behavior and model a way to calm down until you can be respectful.

9. Validate the child's feelings—whatever you think they may be: "You sound so angry." Sometimes you can validate feelings while gently leading the child to what needs to be done.

10. Admit the power struggle and back off. "I can't make you, but I really need your help. Let's both think about a solution and get back together in three minutes."

11. Make sure the message of caring gets through. "I really care about you, and I have faith that we can work this out in ways that are respectful to both of us."

Tips for Working with Parents

Share these suggestions with parents. Many of them will think the suggestions are too time-consuming. Yes, children *are* time-consuming. But these skills are actually less time-consuming than lectures, scolding, nagging, power struggles, and all the various forms of punishment that only increase resistance. These skills also are much more fun to use—and they help children learn valuable life skills.

Motivation, Lack of

Child Development Concept

Young children don't lack motivation to do things they are developmentally programmed to do. They are highly motivated to explore, experiment, discover, and learn from play and from their natural environment. However, adults often have a different agenda. This is not bad—just different. For example, children are motivated to play with toys. Adults want them to be motivated to pick up the toys. We agree that children should be taught to pick up their toys, but to want them to develop an inner motivation to do so will only lead to frustration. Adults need to first accept the fact that children don't have the same priorities that adults have, and then they must get children involved in doing what needs to be done without expecting them to be motivated to do it.

Teachers also wonder how best to motivate a child to learn—to pursue academics, reading, or athletic skills with interest and dedication. Children who lack motivation are often discouraged; they do not believe they can belong in these ways and want adults either to do things for them or to leave them alone. Children who are deeply discouraged need to have their sense of belonging and significance bolstered; they need to be helped to discover small steps, to experience small successes, and to have their self-esteem strengthened with life skills.

Suggestions

1. Accept the fact that you are motivated and find creative ways to involve children without expecting *them* to be motivated. Allowing children some choices about tasks, projects, or other activities may also increase their motivation to work and to succeed.

2. Create routines *with* the children for things that need to be done. (See page 53.) Involving children in the process is one of the best ways to motivate children. They do seem more motivated to follow a plan they have helped create than to follow one that is imposed on them.

3. Decide what you will do (not what you will try to make children do), and then follow through. For example: "I'll read a story as soon as the blocks are picked up." "You can have another bag of toys as soon as the toys on the floor are picked up."

4. Do things (e.g., picking up blocks) *with* children instead of expecting them to do it by themselves.

5. Having children sing songs while they do tasks doesn't really motivate them, but it may make it more pleasant for them to do what needs to be done.

6. Use the words "I need your help." Children are motivated to find belonging and significance and like to be needed. This gives them a sense of belonging and capability.

7. Shut your mouth and act. Instead of telling a child what to do, take her by the hand and gently lead her to what needs to be done. When you get there, you could add, "I need your help to get this job done."

8. Offer choices: "Would you like to pick up the square blocks or the round blocks?" Again, this approach doesn't motivate a child so much as it gives him a sense of power in doing a task he wouldn't otherwise do.

9. Invite the children to use their thinking skills: "What do you think needs to be done before we do what

is next?" They will be more motivated to use their power to think things through than to do the task, but in the process the task is more likely to get done.

10. Do not use rewards. Rewards motivate children to manipulate adults into giving them more rewards rather than allowing them to experience the inner rewards of contribution.

11. Build on strengths. Children, especially deeply discouraged children, often find it easier to get started on something when the task at hand is something they genuinely enjoy or are good at. It may take some work to discover what a child's strengths are, but you are more likely to be successful in motivating him when you begin from a position of strength and encouragement.

Tips for Working with Parents

Help parents understand that children are motivated to use their power—and will do so in useful or useless ways. Adults can help guide them to use their power in useful ways through any of these suggestions. Punishment and rewards only lead to power struggles.

Nap Time (Quiet Time)

Child Development Concept

What a dilemma! Children want and need sleep, and they also want and need to explore and learn. They may resist sleep because they are afraid they will miss something, but because they need sleep, they often become cranky when they miss a nap. Most caregivers know that nap time can easily turn into a power struggle. Many licensing agencies require children under the age of five or so to lie down and rest for a specified period of time; many children (and some parents) insist just as firmly that they don't *need* a nap.

As with so many problems, routines, especially routines created *with* children, can work wonders. It also helps when adults learn how to avoid power struggles.

Suggestions

1. Involve children in the creation of a quiet time routine chart. Let them make a list (with a little dictation from you) about what needs to be done before quiet time. The list might include clean-up, toileting, washing, unfolding their mats, story time, and soft music. Pictures from magazines, children's drawings, or Polaroid pictures of children doing the tasks make the routine chart special.

2. Ask the children to tell you what is next on their quiet time routine chart.

3. Let the children know that they don't have to sleep, but that quiet time should be quiet. Let them

SEESAW ACTIVITY

Objective

To help adults understand how effective it can be to avoid words and power struggles while using kind and firm action. As Rudolf Dreikurs used to say, "Keep your mouth shut and act."

Directions

1. Form dyads. Ask the partners to decide which one will play the child and which one the adult.
2. Give the following instructions: "It is quiet time, and the child gets off the mat and starts wandering around. The adult will go to the child and take him or her by the hand and kindly and firmly lead the child back to the mat. When the child resists, the adult is to use the 'seesaw method.'"
3. Ask for a volunteer to role-play a child so you can demonstrate the seesaw method as follows. Gently pull the child toward the mat. When she resists, stop pulling and let her pull you until she stops. (The child usually stops

choose a book to read while lying on their mats.

4. Invite children to bring their special blankets or stuffed animals. These items can be taken from their cubbies only during quiet time.

5. Sometimes it helps for children to have a back rub. Be sure *you* don't do this, or you may inadvertently encourage children to seek special service from you—and to compete with one another for your attention. Let children take turns giving each other back rubs for three or four minutes. Children can even take turns setting the timer for "back rub time."

6. Don't argue with children who claim they don't need a nap. Agree with them and give them a choice of reading a book or listening to the soft music during the quiet time. If they continue to argue, give them a

pulling very quickly when you don't resist.) Wait a few seconds and then start pulling the child toward the mat. When she resists, stop pulling, as before. Continue doing this (back and forth like a see saw) until the child gives up and follows you to the mat.

4. During this demonstration, the person playing the child usually gives up and follows the adult. (It isn't fun to engage in a power struggle when the other person isn't struggling.) If he or she doesn't give in, stop the demonstration and explain the following: "When role-playing, please be the child, but also be in your body. In other words, do what you think a child might do, but also do what you feel like doing in response to what is being done to you. Most adults play a child who reacts to punishment or control, and they continue to play that child even when the punishment and control is not happening."

5. Now ask the partners to take turns role-playing the adult and the child so they can experience the seesaw method from both positions.

6. When they have finished (a minute or two for each position), invite them to share their experience and what they learned.

smile or a wink and then ignore them. If a child gets up from his mat, kindly and firmly take him by the hand and lead him back to the mat. It is important to keep your mouth shut and your attitude friendly. Talking just gives them fuel to talk back. You may have to kindly and firmly lead them back to the mat several times. (See the seesaw activity in the sidebar.)

Tips for Working with Parents

Parents can benefit from all of these suggestions. It will be especially helpful for them to understand how important it is to "keep your mouth shut" while acting kindly and firmly. If you have the opportunity, involve parents (and staff) in the seesaw activity (see the sidebar).

Separation Anxiety

(See *Clinging* and *Crying*)

Child Development Concept

Separation anxiety is a normal developmental phase during which children become distressed and fearful when their parents leave. Children understand that their parents still exist— they just don't understand why they must leave. This understanding that

their parents still exist makes their separation anxiety stronger because they know their parents are out there somewhere, but they don't understand why their crying doesn't bring them back. Developmentally, children need to feel secure before they can explore the outside world. Attachment security is one of the most important indicators of quality care for infants and toddlers because it builds trust. The children need to become attached to childcare providers to develop this trust.

We believe that children form a sense of trust versus mistrust in the first year (see Erik Erikson's stages of emotional development in chapter 4), but we differ from some theorists about how to help children develop trust. Some "experts" believe that carrying a baby around all the time, never leaving the baby with a stranger, and sleeping with the baby is the best way to develop trust. We do not agree. This may be counterproductive to the development of self-trust and may lead to excessive dependence on others. Yes, babies must depend on others, but the goal of parents and caregivers is to help them develop a sense of trust in themselves—including the experience that they can handle disappointment and anxiety.

Research has shown that babies can thrive when they receive love at home and love in a quality childcare situation. Quality childcare can provide an extended community that reinforces the lessons of trust, connection, and respect.

Suggestions:

1. Have faith in children to survive separation so long as they are provided with love and support, both at home and in the childcare environment—and that some will adjust sooner than others.

2. A transitional object from home, such as a toy, blanket, or a mother's shirt (if the child is breastfeeding), will sometimes help.

3. Request that a parent spend at least several hours with his or her child while the child gets familiar with your childcare environment. We know this could be a hardship for a parent who has to work, and it may not be possible. However, it is worth the investment of time if it is possible.

4. After the initial adjustment period, if a child is still having difficulty separating, ask the parent to leave as soon as possible and then hold the child on your lap for a while, or rock the child if possible. If you cannot provide this comfort because you have too many other children who cannot entertain themselves, do not accept infants or toddlers.

5. The reason we suggest asking the parent to leave as soon as possible is that some children use this situation (as they get older) to seek undue attention or misguided power. We are not saying the separation anxiety isn't real, but that it can develop into something else (such as manipulation or misbehavior) when adults don't handle the situation with calm and confidence

6. Understand that children have needs and wants. They may want their mother, but they *need* love and a safe environment. Of course, children should have their wants met sometimes (shouldn't we all), but catering to *every* want can produce a very

self-centered child. It takes knowledge and sensitivity to understand the difference between separation anxiety (a need) and manipulation (a want).

7. A child with a slow-to-warm temperament type may have much more difficulty with separation anxiety. Remember that some children take longer than others. Childcare providers should be patient and loving with these children and help parents understand the stage.

Tips for Working with Parents

Parents often feel heartbroken and guilty when their children suffer from separation anxiety. Their guilt only exacerbates the problem. Share with them the information provided above with the hope that it might ease their guilt and help them to understand that the process of coping with separation is part of every child's normal developmental challenges.

Sometimes children become attached to their childcare provider and do not want to leave to go with their parents. These children usually adjust to their parents very quickly once they leave the childcare environment. Parents should be grateful, instead of jealous, that their children have become attached to the childcare provider and feel secure while away from their parents.

Sharing

Child Development Concept

Suppose you have four three-year-olds going out to play. On the playground you have exactly one tricycle. "Share the tricycle," you tell them optimistically, before heading indoors for a moment. What do you suppose will happen?

If you guessed "pandemonium," you win the prize. The ability to share is one of the most sophisticated social skills human beings acquire in life, and children need time, encouragement, and teaching to learn it. Children who cannot or do not share are not "selfish" or "self-centered"; they are not yet developmentally able to take the wishes of others into consideration. Because young children are egocentric (i.e., they are the cen-

ter of their own universe and are not yet able to respect the needs and feelings of others), they want what they want, and they want it *now*. They are not capable of understanding a balance—that it is nice to share sometimes, but you don't have to share all the time. Adults often expect children to share all the time, when adults don't have such high expectations for themselves.

Suggestions

1. Encourage children to "use their words." For example, if two boys are wrestling for possession of the red dump truck, help them find ways to talk about sharing it (rather than scolding them or grabbing the truck yourself). You might say, "Sam, can

you ask Mark if you can use the truck?" Sam might ask, perhaps throwing in a grab or a grumble for good measure. You can then help Mark find kind, respectful ways to respond.

2. Consider teaching children to use a simple kitchen timer and to agree about how long each of them may use a particular toy. Young children often love to hold the timer and wait for the beep, and the distraction can make waiting for their turn easier to endure.

3. Have a class meeting and put "sharing" on the agenda. Because all young children must learn this important skill, involving them in discovering ways to practice kindness and respect is a marvelous way to teach—and to reduce the amount of refereeing caregivers must do.

4. Model sharing for children. Say, "I have a cookie. I'll have a bite, and then I'll share a piece with you. Can you share with me, too?"

5. Recognize that sharing is a complex social skill, and it takes time and a great deal of practice to perfect it. Punishment, lectures, or nagging is

SUCCESSFUL STRATEGIES FOR TEACHING YOUNG CHILDREN TO SHARE

- Understand that sharing is an abstract concept that is developmentally beyond the capability of children to understand before the age of three or four. They may mimic sharing before this, but that doesn't mean they understand it. You can still take time for training until the concept is absorbed, but don't have expectations beyond a child's capability.

- Model sharing yourself by saying, "I want to share my cake with you" or "Let's take turns bouncing the ball. I'll count to ten while you bounce it, then we'll count to ten while I bounce it."

- Let children know they don't have to share everything all the time. Ask, "What toy do you want to share, and which one to you want to keep for yourself?"

- Use words to coach children in the art of respectful negotiation. Demonstration is often the most effective teaching tool for preschoolers.

- Give opportunities for sharing and taking turns. Say, "I know that's your favorite toy. Which toy would you be willing to share with Michael?" or "You can go first at 'Chutes and Ladders,' and Aaron can go first at 'Cootie.'"

- Acknowledge children's feelings. When children have difficulty sharing, validate their feelings by saying, "I know it can be hard to share (or take turns). I have faith that you will do it when you are ready."

- Avoid judging or shaming children by labeling them as "selfish" or "naughty," or by forcing an apology. Doing so does not encourage respect or sharing.

unlikely to motivate children to share; patient teaching will usually do the trick—over time, when children are developmentally ready.

Tips for Working with Parents

As with so many other aspects of a young child's behavior, parents need help in understanding that social skills such as sharing take time to develop, that egocentricity is normal for young children, and that teaching and modeling are the best ways to cultivate this skill. It may also be helpful to remind parents not to allow children to bring special toys from home; other children will want to play with them, too. There is no need to invite power struggles over sharing when they're not absolutely necessary. Give parents the additional strategies listed in the sidebar for teaching about sharing.

Staff Changes

Child Development Concept

Few things cause more disruption for young children in childcare than when a favorite teacher must leave them or when children themselves must move from one group or class to another. Caregivers are vitally important to young children; they create a sense of belonging, offer caring and affection, and are among a child's first teachers and mentors. Saying good-bye is difficult, and it is not un-usual for children's behavior to deteriorate in the wake of staff or class changes. Staff changes are inevitable, but there are ways to ease the transition for you and for the children.

Suggestions

1. As much as possible, let children know that a change is coming. Give them time to ask questions, to express their feelings, and to accept the idea of change. Children often are most comfortable when they experience consistency and routine, so changes are inherently difficult.

2. Allow a child's "old" teacher and the new teacher to work together with the children for a day or two. Children can experience a gradual transition and can see that their new teacher understands their routines and ways of doing things. This can also make it easier for new staff members, who have time to learn children's names and to understand class meetings, kind and firm discipline, and other Positive Discipline principles.

3. Have a special class meeting or circle time and invite children to offer a compliment or appreciation to their departing teacher. Children may enjoy making a good-bye card, in which they can draw pictures or sign their names.

4. Let children know that their new teacher will need their help. Children like to be included and involved; feeling like "consultants" may avoid power struggles and boundary testing while the new teacher settles in.

Tips for Working with Parents

Parents, too, need to be informed of staff changes, because their children may ask questions or express feelings at home. Parents sometimes see a change in behavior while children adjust to a new teacher or a new routine. In-home caregivers can also adapt the suggestions offered here to help parents and children when they must move to a new childcare facility.

Strong-Willed Child

Child Development Concept

Many children these days are labeled as "strong-willed," and it's rarely intended as a compliment. We would like to suggest another possibility. Children simply do what works. What they really want is to belong, to feel capable, and to have a sense of personal power. When children don't feel a sense of belonging, they will choose a *mistaken* way to gain that sense. The reason it is called a *mistaken* way is that they will choose a way that they mistakenly believe will help them feel belonging and significance, but isn't useful to themselves or others. For example, some children mistakenly believe they will belong if they get *undue attention, misguided power,* or *revenge* (hurting back because they don't believe they belong and that hurts), or they *give up*. (See information on the mistaken goals of misbehavior in chapter 3.)

Children who are labeled as strong-willed have usually chosen the mistaken goal of misguided power. Remember, too, that children have different temperaments and may vary in their perseverance, aggressiveness, or activity level. Teachers sometimes label a child "strong-willed" (meaning defiant) when the child's temperament is not a good fit with the teacher's own.

An adult's job is to help these children use their strong wills to be helpful and to make a contribution in their world.

Suggestions

1. Instead of focusing on the behavior of the child, adults will be most effective if they focus on their own behavior. Look for ways to help the child feel belonging by helping her feel capable and by guiding her to use her power in useful ways.

2. Notice, also, if you are being too controlling, giving too many orders, or engaging in other behaviors that invite rebellion.

3. Let the child help and give him limited choices: "Do you want to put on your shirt first or your pants? You

decide." That "You decide" is very important to help a child feel a sense of useful power, even though it is limited. Many children resist (become strong-willed) when bossed around. They become motivated and cooperative (strong-willed in a positive way) when they are respectfully involved.

4. Ask "what" and "how" questions (page 62): "What do you need to do before you are ready to leave?" It is amazing how much more cooperative a child may feel when he is asked instead of told.

5. Do *not* give rewards for appropriate behavior. Rewards take away from the development of a sense of capability and will instead teach children to do things only for the reward (instead of being a cooperative member of the family or group). Rewards usually seem to work for a while, but then they create power struggles and manipulation. This is because rewards don't help children feel a sense of belonging or competence, nor do they teach children to use their autonomy usefully.

Tips for Working with Parents

It may be a shock for parents to think about the possibility of changing their behavior instead of focusing on the behavior of their children, yet what a gift to the children. A gentle way to put this is to share your own experience. Let parents know that you have learned that a misbehaving child is a discouraged child and that when you find ways to encourage that child, the behavior changes. Also, point out that a strong will can be a valuable quality, especially as the child grows to adulthood, when guided in a positive direction.

Tattling

Child Development Concept

Adults get upset when children tattle (so do other children), but they usually don't realize that children tattle for three main reasons:

1. They don't have the skills to solve problems.

2. Adults encourage tattling by rescuing children or lecturing about not tattling instead of teaching problem-solving skills.

3. Children think they can receive attention and make themselves look good by making another child look bad.

Instead of being annoyed by tattling, welcome it as an opportunity to encourage children through the development of problem-solving skills.

Suggestions

1. When a child comes to you to tattle, first use active listening to acknowledge the child's feelings—whatever you think they might be.

2. Once children feel understood, they are more open to learning. Sometimes this learning can take place from their inner process. In other words, listen to and acknowledge the child's

feelings without thinking you have to do anything else. Feeling understood is often enough to start the inner learning process.

3. After listening, ask the child, "What do you think would solve this problem so everyone would be happy?" If the child says, "I don't know," respond with, "You are good thinker, so why don't you think about it and let me know when you have an idea."

4. Ask the child to make an appointment with the child she is talking about so they can work together on a solution.

5. Show faith in the child by saying, "I have faith in you to find a respectful way to solve this problem."

6. Ask, "How is this a problem for you?" If the child can tell you how the problem affects her, then try one of the previous suggestions. If the problem does not involve the child, and the situation is not dangerous, you might say, "Hmmmm. I wonder how those involved will solve the problem." If it is a dangerous problem, rush to protect the children from danger and later thank the child for her help.

7. When you are having class or group meetings, you can ask children four years old and older to put the problem on the agenda so the whole group can brainstorm for solutions.

8. These suggestions don't mean that you should never help a child. Listen to your intuition; be aware that sometimes a problem is beyond a child's ability to handle and that he genuinely needs your help.

9. Find opportunities to teach problem-solving skills during conflict-free times. Class meetings provide an excellent opportunity for children to learn problem-solving skills.

Tips for Working with Parents

Often parents encourage tattling by getting too involved in solving children's problems for them. They may encourage competition and the tendency for their children to try to make themselves look good by making their siblings look bad when they take sides in a fight.

Encourage parents to help their children focus on solutions by inviting their children to use the Wheel of Choice (page 164) or Anger Wheel of Choice (page 133) or to put the problem on the family meeting agenda.

Toilet Training

Child Development Concept

The first thought that came to us while writing this topic was "Much ado about nothing." Why has a natural bodily function become such a major battlefield?

In our book *Positive Discipline for Preschoolers,* we have a section titled "Sleeping, Eating, and Toileting—You Can't Make 'Em Do It." Aw, there's the rub. The reason toilet training has become a battlefield is that adults keep trying to "make" children do things they would naturally do without adult interference—eventually.

It is wise to remember that while the ability to use the toilet (and leave those messy, smelly diapers behind forever) is convenient for adults, children must be physically ready for this grown-up skill. Some children are slower than others to recognize the tingling or full feeling that is meant to tell them it's time to "go." Other children discover, quite accurately, that leaving their play, having to deal with buttons, zippers, and snaps, and using the bathroom are time-consuming—and decide to stay in diapers as long as possible. The average age for toilet training today is between three and three-and-a-half years of age; some caregivers believe it is getting even later because diapers are becoming more comfortable and absorbent, and children are unlikely to feel discomfort even when their diapers are soiled.

Why do children learn a language? Because they mimic what they see happening in their world. Adults don't seem to get nearly as obsessed with teaching language as they do with toilet training. They seem to *know* language will happen eventually. As a wise pediatrician once said, "Children never go off to kindergarten in diapers." Time, patience, and opportunity usually solve the problem without excessive adult intervention.

Toileting (along with eating and sleeping) is one of those areas that intelligent little people soon learn is a great place to test their autonomy and personal power. After all, where else can they feel and see how much commotion they can create by simply refusing to do what adults think they have the power to make them do?

Suggestions

1. Relax! Take comfort in knowing that children are likely to be taking care of their own toileting by the time they go to college. Avoid power

struggles by giving up your need to have power over the child's natural bodily functions.

2. Childcare providers have an excellent opportunity to assist with toilet training because they are not as emotionally involved as parents. They also have the advantage of routines and other children who are modeling socially acceptable toileting. We know you don't look forward to changing poopy diapers, but every job provides pleasures and "yuk" work. The poopy diapers won't last long when you proceed as follows.

3. Understand age appropriateness. If you are caring for infants, you must accept that poopy diapers are part of the job. Understand individual developmental time lines. Children between the ages of two to four will become toilet trained at different times. Do not compare children. Girls usually become toilet trained sooner than boys. Any child who is not toilet trained by age four may have a medical problem—or a power-happy adult in their life.

4. Your attitude is the key ingredient. If children sense you don't have any personal investment (power or control issues) in their toileting, they won't be called to battle. Be unconcerned.

5. It is okay to require "pull-ups" for children two and older. Pull-ups make it easier for children to engage in the toilet training process and to help clean themselves (see step 8) when they have accidents.

6. Include toilet times in your regular routines. Provide times when all the children go to the bathroom area. If you have a center with many small toilets, several children can use the toilet at the same time. If you provide childcare in your home, invest in a few small potty chairs so some can be using them while others are waiting their turn (and observing lots of modeling).

7. Take time for training. Show children the toileting routine, and then watch while they do it. Show them (or let an older child) show them how to use toilet paper and how to drop it in the toilet, how to empty potty seats into the big toilet, how to flush, and how to wash their hands when finished.

8. Some children may need training in how to help clean themselves when they have an accident. Parents can bring one or two changes of clothing. You can have several small washcloths or a box of wipes available. Take time for training in how to remove their

soiled pull-ups, put them in a special plastic bag, wash themselves off (with help, if needed), and put on their change of clothes. All of this should be done calmly and kindly, without blame, shame, or pain.

9. You might include songs the children sing while engaging in the toileting routine. For instance, the following (sung to the tune of "Skip to My Lou") can be sung while washing hands. When repeated twice, the song lasts about 20 seconds—just the time it takes to kill *E. coli* bacteria.

Wash, wash, wash your hands,
Wash your hands together.
Scrub, scrub, scrub your hands,
'Til they're clean and sparkly.

10. Do not use rewards or praise. These are invitations to power struggles, and children should not be taught that there is anything special about taking care of normal bodily functions.

Tips for Working with Parents

Share some of these suggestions with parents. It will be especially helpful for

---

FLUSHING THE POWER STRUGGLE

One of the authors found an excellent preschool, Tot Town, for her two-year-old son, Mark, when it was time for her to go back to work. Mark was not toilet trained, and Mom was feeling desperate. Much to her relief, the director said, "Don't worry about it. We will have him toilet trained very quickly because it is part of our routine, and children like to do what other children are doing. We don't do the toilet training—the other children do."

The interesting thing about this story is that Mark had very few accidents at Tot Town, but he still had lots of "accidents" at home. It took Mom several months to realize that her "concern" about his toileting was inviting a power struggle. When she gave up her concern and followed procedures like those in this chapter's suggestions, Mark was soon "toilet trained"—at home as well as at school.

them to see how they may be inviting power struggles over toileting. They will also be extremely relieved by your attitude of "nonconcern" and willingness to include toilet training as part of your program instead of insisting the child be toilet trained (talk about added pressure and more fuel for power struggles at home) before being part of your program.

Whining

(see also *Crying*)

Child Development Concept

Children would not whine if it didn't work. What kind of response does whining provoke from you? Children can learn any language depending on the culture into which they are born, and whining seems to be common to most cultures—if it works.

Just like crying, whining is another language, but it certainly is an annoying one. Whining can be used to get undue attention or to gain misguided power—if it works. Whining is a very manipulative language—if it works. Once you get the "if it works" part, you will find that most suggestions are related to having you stop your reactive behavior instead of trying to get the child to stop whining. After all, the only person you can truly control is yourself.

Suggestions

1. Respond to the child instead of to the whining. See the discouragement and offer some encouragement. You might say, "Sounds like you need a hug" or "I'll bet you can figure out what to do."

2. When you change your attitude about whining, it will be easier to change your response. Instead of letting the whining "work," you might smile at the child and then turn your attention to something else. You don't have to fix everything, and

children are likely to stop doing what doesn't work.

3. Without reacting to the whining, simply state what you think the child might be trying to say: "You would like my help. You can use your words and ask for my help," or "I know you want that toy. Billy has it now," or "Billy took the toy from you. What do you need to tell him?" A matter-of-fact attitude will be effective. Expressing your own annoyance won't. Children often will settle for negative attention if they can't get positive attention, and your irritation with their whining may be good enough for them.

4. If you can't change your attitude and whining still annoys you, it is okay to be honest about that feeling. During a calm time, you might tell the child that you don't like to listen to whining, so you will cover your ears when you hear whining (or will walk away) and that you would love to listen when the child is ready to talk in a normal voice. (It is helpful to smile and be kind when you say this— doing anything to shame or embarrass a child will not solve the problem.)

5. Use your sense of humor: "Here comes the tickle monster to tickle children who whine."

6. Remember that a misbehaving child is a discouraged child. Many things can be discouraging, including a lack of skills. Find ways to encourage and teach skills such as asking for what you want.

Tips for Working with Parents

At home, children whine about their siblings and about wanting things in the store; as one parent said, "They whine about just about everything." Let parents know that children do only what works and share some of these suggestions. Let them know that it may be more difficult for them to be objective about whining because they are more emotionally involved and may have a difficult time acting instead of reacting. It can be comforting to know that this response is normal.

"PLAY TOGETHER" ART RECIPES

Bubble Brew

10 parts water to 1 part liquid detergent
(Joy or Dawn seem to make the best bubbles!)

Measure all ingredients in a recycled, clean, plastic pail; let stand, covered, overnight. Pour mixture into a styrofoam cup and insert a straw or coffee stirrer at an angle near the cup's top. Sit children at the table over a dishpan on a towel. Or pour into a dishpan, take outdoors, and make BIG bubble-blowers using kitchen utensils like clean fly swatters, berry baskets, six-pack rings, pipe cleaners (make ◇▯□, and observe how the bubbles are always round), single-sided cheese grater, pancake turners, slotted spoons. Empty toilet paper tubes also make good blowers. Put bubble-blowers in the tub; or with a plastic table-cloth on the floor, have child sit in the middle of the cloth or stand on a safe step-stool at the kitchen sink with an apron on.

Finger Paint #1—Cooked Paint

1 1/2 cups corn starch
7 cups boiling water
cold water
1 1/2 cups soap flakes
food coloring

Mix starch with enough cold water to make a paste. Add to boiling water and cook until glossy. Stir in soap flakes while mixture is still warm. Add food coloring, and stir to mix well. Keeps for a week if tightly covered.

Finger Paint #2

shaving cream or hand lotion (Travel size is just right! Use non-scented if child has allergies. Add food coloring powdered tempera if desired)

Squirt some onto a cookie sheet or freezer paper. Write with your finger, draw something, and smooth out the shaving cream/lotion like a magic slate and start all over! Add salt for texture and a glistening finish.

Puff Squeeze Paint

Mix equal parts flour, salt, and water. 2 cups of each ingredient makes enough mixture for four colors. Add 1 tablespoon powdered tempera for each color desired. Spoon into plastic squeeze bottles. Squeeze mixture onto the paper to form a design; thoroughly dry before hanging up the finished painting.

Water Painting

Plastic buckets, clear if you can get them
Disposable paint pans, big brushes and rollers

Fill the buckets with water. Add food coloring if desired. Use the rollers and brushes to "paint the town!" (sidewalks, driveways, buildings).

Saltwater Paint

Sprinkle salt over still-wet water-painting for a new look!

Baggie Painting

Put 2 tablespoons of one color homemade fingerpaint or one tablespoon of three colors (red, yellow, blue) into a baggie and zip shut.

Invite children to squeeze the bag or write with a finger on the bag. Discuss the textures, lines, and colors mixed.

Crayon/Marker/Colored Pencil Fun

Rubber band three or four crayons together and invite your child to make "scribble" pictures by going 'round and 'round on paper with these crayons. The shapes formed can then be colored in as desired.

Try banding together a marker, a colored pencil, and a crayon, inviting children to explore the thicknesses of the marks, the colors, and the interesting lines these three materials make.

Melted Crayon Chunks

Save crayon pieces; store in a can without the papers. When the can is full, fill the cups of an old muffin pan with the pieces and melt in a slow oven (150 degrees). Be sure you include some of the lighter colors, so the chunks are not too dark. Let the melted crayon solidify and cool—now make interesting crayon pictures. A good way to recycle broken crayons.

Slime

Begin with 3 cups cornstarch and $1/2$ cup water in a jelly-roll pan or cookie sheet with a lip. Add water by dribbles, until the texture you desire appears. Mixture should flow from fingertips. Add food color if desired. Children enjoy the feel of this exploratory material. Save to re-use in a clean, recycled peanut-butter jar. Add more water if mixture dries out. This mixture lasts a long time.

Homemade Paste

1 cup cold water

1 cup flour

$2 1/4$ cup boiling water

1 teaspoon alum

$3/4$ teaspoon wintergreen flavoring

Mix cold water with flour, stirring until smooth. Stir and add boiling water, cooking over low heat until smooth and a shiny bluish gray color. Add flavoring if desired for a fresh smell. Store in fridge for long-lasting, inexpensive paste.

Play Dough

#1 Favorite cooked play-dough

1 cup flour

1 cup water

1 tablespoon cooking oil

$^1/_2$ cup salt

food coloring

a few drops

1 tablespoon cream of tartar

Mix all ingredients and cook over medium-low heat, stirring with a wooden spoon, drawing the dough into a ball as it cooks. Cool. Knead on a floured surface 'til smooth. Store in a sealed container; refrigerate and keep indefinitely. Make the three primary colors and encourage child to mix orange, green, and purple.

#2 Uncooked Play Dough

water, begin with $^1/_2$ cup and slowly add more as needed

2 cups flour

1 cup salt

2 tablespoon cooking oil

4 teaspoons cream of tartar

Mix well. Add a few drops of food coloring to the water; knead until smooth, Keep in covered container; add more flour when it gets sticky; keep about two to three weeks.

#3 Cinnamon Play Dough

2 cups flour

1 tablespoon cooking oil

2 cups water

4 tablespoons cinnamon

2 cups salt

4 tablespoons cream of tartar

Combine all ingredients in saucepan; cook over medium heat until rubbery. Knead on floured surface until smooth. (This dough smells like cinnamon rolls, but with the extra salt, it doesn't taste as good as it smells!) Cool. Store in covered container in fridge indefinitely.

#4 "Sweet-Smelling" Play Dough

1 cup flour

1/2 cup salt

3 tablespoons oil

1 cup boiling water

1 small pkg. unsweetened. powdered juice mix

Add boiling water and oil to dry ingredients. Stir together; knead mixture on floured surface until a ball forms. Notice the interesting texture and smell. Store in covered container in fridge indefinitely. Use several different flavors and store separately. Recycled butter plastic containers make for great play dough storage.

Accessories for Play Dough Fun

Cookie sheet, rolling pin, cookie cutters, blunt table knives and forks, clothespins, craft sticks, film canisters, pipe cleaners, plastic straws, potato masher, spray can lids, toilet paper rolls, toothpicks (if no younger children are around); small muffin/bread pans, plastic containers, small blocks, wooden spools, coffee stir sticks, meat trays, small tiles, aluminum foil pans, small cutting board.

How to Play with Play Dough

Children usually love messy activities; make a rule together that play dough stays on the tray on the table. Remove the dough if your child forgets, and say gently, "We'll try again later." Say "What an interesting texture; blue's your favorite color, isn't it?" Providing interesting accessories can help your child be creative without turning your kitchen into a disaster zone!

Used by permission of Mary L. Hughes, Family Life Field Specialist, Iowa State University Extension

NATIONAL ASSOCIATION FOR THE EDUCATION OF YOUNG CHILDREN STANDARDS AND ACCREDITATION

THE NATIONAL ASSOCIATION for the Education of Young Children (NAEYC) is the nation's largest (and probably most influential) organization of early childhood educators and other caregivers, who are dedicated to improving the quality of programs for children from birth through third grade. Founded in 1926, NAEYC has over 100,000 members and a national network of nearly 450 local, state, and regional affiliates. The NAEYC offers an annual conference, conducts research, and promotes high standards of quality in order to ensure that children receive the best possible care while in a childcare setting.

Perhaps one of the most important services provided by NAEYC is the formation of standards for childcare accreditation. Accreditation is not simple, but it does lead to higher standards in both care and staff education and training. You may want to consider becoming an NAEYC accredited program. Accreditation involves three steps: self-study, validation, and an accreditation decision. Detailed information is available from the NAEYC at 1509 16th Street NW, Washington, D.C., 20036-1426; at (800) 424-2460; or at their website (www .naeyc.org). Even if you choose not to pursue accreditation, these standards may give you ideas about how you can create a high-quality program for the children you care for.

A summary of accreditation standards is provided below:

Interactions Among Teachers and Children

INTERACTIONS BETWEEN CHILDREN and adults provide opportunities for children to develop an understanding of self and others and are characterized by warmth, personal respect, individuality, positive support, and responsiveness. Teachers facilitate interactions among children to provide opportunities for development of self-esteem, social competence, and intellectual growth.

• Teachers are available and responsive to children; encourage them to share experiences, ideas, and feelings; and listen to them with attention and respect.

• Teachers treat children of all races, religions, family backgrounds, and cultures with equal respect and consideration.

• Teachers abstain from corporal punishment or humiliating or frightening discipline techniques.

• Teachers support children's emotional development, assisting children to be comfortable, relaxed, happy, and involved in play and other activities.

Curriculum

THE CURRICULUM INCLUDES the goals of the program (the content that children are learning) and the planned activities as well as the daily schedule, the availability and use of material, transitions between activities, and the way in which routine tasks of living are used as learning experiences. Criteria for curriculum implementation reflect the knowledge that young children are active learners, drawing on direct physical and social experiences as well as culturally transmitted knowledge to construct their understanding of the world around them.

• The program has a written statement of its philosophy and goals for children which is available to all staff and families.

• The program has written curriculum plans on knowledge of child development and learning, and assessment of individual needs and interests.

• Developmentally appropriate materials and equipment are available to infants, toddlers, preschoolers, kindergartners, and school-age children.

• Routine tasks are incorporated into the program as a means of furthering children's learning, self-help, and social skills.

Relationships Among Teachers and Families

TEACHERS AND FAMILIES work closely in partnership to ensure high-quality care and education for children, and parents feel supported and welcomed as observers and contributors to the program.

• A process has been developed for orienting children and families to the program that may include a pre-enrollment visit, parent orientation meeting, or gradual introduction of children to the program that also supports children and families through the separation process.

• Teachers work in collaborative partnerships with families, establishing and maintaining regular, ongoing two-way communication with children's parents to build trust and mutual understanding, and to ensure that children's learning and developmental needs are met. Teachers listen to parents, seek to understand their goals and preferences for their children, and respect cultural and family differences.

• Administrators and teachers are familiar with and make appropriate use of community resources including social services; mental and physical health agencies; and education programs such as museums, libraries, and neighborhood centers.

Staff Qualifications and Professional Development

THE PROGRAM IS staffed by adults who understand child and family development and who recognize and meet the developmental and learning needs of children and families.

• Staff who work directly with children are 18 years of age or older and demonstrate the appropriate personal characteristics for working with children as exemplified in NAEYC criteria.

• Early childhood teacher assistants (staff who implement program activities under direct supervision) are high school graduates or the equivalent, have been trained in Early Childhood Education/Child Development, and/or participate in ongoing professional development programs.

• Early Childhood Teachers (staff who are responsible for the care and education of a group of children from birth through age 5) have *at least* an associate degree in Early Childhood Development/Child Development, or an equivalent credential.

• The administrator has expertise (acquired through formal education and experience) in both Early Childhood Education/Child Development and administration such as Human Resource and Financial Management.

• In programs serving infants, toddlers, preschoolers, and/or kindergartners, an Early Childhood Specialist (an individual with *at least* a baccalaureate degree in Early Childhood Education/Child Development and three years of full-time teaching experience with young children and/or a graduate degree in Early Childhood Education/Child Development) is employed to direct the educational program (may be the director or other appropriate person, such as Education Coordinator, Curriculum Specialist, or Assistant Director).

Administration

THE PROGRAM IS efficiently and effectively administered with attention to the needs and desires of children, families, and staff.

• The program has written policies and procedures for operating, fees, illness, holidays, refund information, and termination of enrollment.

• Benefits packages for full-time staff include paid leave, medical insurance, and retirement.

• In cases where the program is governed by a board of directors, the program has written policies defining roles and responsibilities of board members and staff.

• Fiscal records are kept with evidence of long-range budgeting and sound financial planning.

Staffing

THE PROGRAM IS sufficiently staffed to meet the needs of and promote the physical, social, emotional, and cognitive development of children.

Recommended maximum staff-child ratios within group size:

AGE OF CHILDREN	MAXIMUM GROUP SIZE	RATIOS
Infants (birth to 12 months)	8	1:4
Toddlers (12 to 24 months)	12 10	1:4 1:5
2-year-olds (24 to 30 months)	12	1:6
2^1/2-year-olds (30 to 36 months)	14	1:7
3-year-olds	20	1:10
4-year-olds	20	1:10
5-year-olds	20	1:10
Kindergartners	24	1:12
6- to 8-year-olds	30	1:15
9- to 12-year-olds	30	1:15

Physical Environment

THE INDOOR AND outdoor physical environment fosters optimal growth and development through opportunities for exploration and learning.

- There is a minimum of 35 square feet of usable playroom floor space per child indoors.
- There is a minimum of 75 square feet of play space outdoors per child.
- A variety of age-appropriate materials and equipment are available for children indoors and outdoors.
- A variety of activities can go on outdoors throughout the year.
- The work environment for staff, including classrooms and staff rooms, is comfortable, well-organized, and in good repair.

Health and Safety

THE HEALTH AND safety of children and adults are protected and enhanced.

- The program presents valid certification that it is in compliance with all legal requirements for protection of health and safety of children in group settings, such as building codes, sanitation, water quality, and fire protection. The program is licensed or accredited to operate by the appropriate state/local agencies.
- A current, written record is maintained for each child, including the results of a complete health evaluation by an approved health care resource within six months prior to enrollment, record of immunizations, emergency contact information, names of people authorized to pick up the child, and pertinent health history.
- Children are under adult supervision at all times.
- Suspected incidents of child abuse and/or neglect by families, staff, volunteers, or others are reported to the appropriate local agencies.
- Program provides certification that nontoxic building materials, no lead paint or asbestos, are used in the facility.
- All pieces of equipment are surrounded by a resilient surface of an acceptable depth or by rubber mats manufactured for such use, consistent with guidelines of the Consumer Product Safety Commission and the Standards of the American Society for Testing and Materials, external limits of the piece of equipment for at least four feet beyond the fall zone.

Nutrition and Food Service

THE NUTRITIONAL NEEDS of children and adults are met in a manner that promotes physical, social, emotional, and cognitive development.

- Meals and snacks are planned to meet the child's nutritional requirements in proportion to the amount of time the child is in the program each day, as recommended by the Child Care Food Program of the U.S. Department of Agriculture.

- Written menus are provided for families.
- Foods indicative of children's cultural backgrounds are served periodically.
- Mealtime is a pleasant social and learning experience for children.

Evaluation

SYSTEMATIC ASSESSMENT OF the effectiveness of the program in meeting its goals for children, families, and staff is conducted to ensure that good quality care and education are provided and maintained, and that the program continually strives for improvement and innovation.

- All staff, including the program administrator, are evaluated at least annually by the director or other appropriate supervisor.
- At least annually, administrators, families, staff, school-age children, and other routinely participating adults are involved in evaluating the program's effectiveness in meeting the needs of children and families.

(Copyright 2002 National Association for the Education of Young Children)

EARLY CHILDHOOD RESOURCES

Active Learning Series by Debbie Cryer, Thelma Harms, and Beth Bourland
Books for curriculum ideas from infancy through 5 years of age.
Order through Redleaf Press: www.redleafpress.org or at 800-423-8309.

Creative Expression Books by Bev Bos
Don't Move the Muffin Tins and others
Turn the Page Press
203 Baldwin Avenue
Roseville, CA 95678
800-959-5549

Chinaberry Catalog
Books of every sort for people who *love* books!
Chinaberry, Inc.
2780 Via Orange Way, Suite B
Spring Valley, CA 91978
800-776-2242
www.chinaberry.com

Creative Curriculum Series by Diane Trister-Dodge
Practical Developmentally Appropriate Practice Ideas, available from Red Leaf
Press.

Creative Resources by Judy Herr
A great "first" curriculum guide—has many basics, but also gets the beginning
teacher thinking about how to plan learning centers. Search www.amazon
.com, where you can purchase new or used books.

Discount School Supply
Ideas and materials, arts & crafts, children's books, curriculum books, affordable equipment for centers/homes.
1-800-627-2829
www.earlychildhood.com

Problem-Solving Series Books for Preschoolers by Elizabeth Crary
I Want It and other titles
Parenting Press, Inc.
P.O. Box 75267,
Seattle, WA 98125
800-992-6657

M.S. Creations Publication Catalog
Every kind of puppet imaginable, books, science and nature learning, teacher resources, videos, storytelling props, and some manipulatives that are quite unique. (We especially love their finger puppets)
1-888-352-8367
www.m-s-creations.com

Warren, Jean.
Animal Piggyback Songs (Warren Publishing House, Inc: Everett, WA, 1990)
Includes "Rabbit Hopping Song," "Bunny-Pokey," "My Rabbit," and "See the Fluffy Rabbit."

Wilmes, Liz and Dick
Curriculum Books—available anywhere. A favorite is *Learning Centers* (ISBN: 0943452139); paperback list price: $19.95
Publisher: Building Blocks, 38 W 567 Brindlewood; Elgin, IL 60123; 800-233-2448

Early Childhood Themes Through the Year by Debbie Thompson.
Teacher Created Materials: www.teachercreated.com

INDEX

ABOUT THE AUTHORS

**Jane Nelsen** is a popular lecturer and coauthor of the entire POSITIVE DISCIPLINE series. She also wrote *From Here to Serenity: Four Principles for Understanding Who You Really Are.* She has appeared on *Oprah* and *Sally Jesse Raphael* and was the featured parent expert on the "National Parent Quiz," hosted by Ben Vereen. Jane is the mother of seven children and the grandmother of eighteen.

**Cheryl Erwin** is a licensed marriage and family therapist in private practice, a lecturer and trainer, and the coauthor of four books in the POSITIVE DISCIPLINE series. Cheryl also has a weekly radio broadcast on parenting in the Reno, Nevada, area, where she lives with her husband and teenaged son.

FOR MORE INFORMATION

THE AUTHORS ARE available for lectures, workshops, and seminars for parents, parent educators, therapists, psychologists, social workers, nurses, counselors, school administrators, teachers, and corporations. (Lectures can be tailored to fit your needs.)

Workshops include:

Positive Discipline in the Classroom (a two-day workshop or a one-day inservice)

Teaching Parenting the Positive Discipline Way (a two-day workshop)

Workshops, seminars, and facilitator training are scheduled throughout the United States each year. To find a location near you or to bring a workshop to your area, contact:

Jane Nelsen
Positive Discipline Associates
969 W. Harmony Rose Circle
So. Jordan, UT 84095
1-800-456-7770
JaneNelsen@aol.com

Cheryl Erwin
3950 Gibraltar Drive
Reno, NV 89509
1-775-826-0327
clerwin@thoughtstream.net

View www.positivediscipline.com for featured articles, answers to parent and teacher questions, and workshop and research information.

Raise a Confident and Capable Child with the *Positive Discipline* Series

In this completely updated edition of *Positive Discipline A-Z*, will give you an overview on using kind but firm support to raise a child who is responsible, respectful, and resourceful. You'll find practical solutions to such parenting challenges as:

sibling rivalry · bedtime hassles · school problems · getting chores done · ADD · eating problems · procrastination · whining · tattling and lying · homework battles · and dozens more!

This newly revised and expanded third edition contains up-to-the-minute information on sleeping through the night, back talk, and lack of motivation as well as tips on diet, exercise, and obesity prevention, and new approaches to parenting in the age of computers and cell phones.

Positive Discipline A-Z

Also in the Positive Discipline *Series*

The Acclaimed Bestseller That Can Improve Your Classroom Experience

Over the years, millions of parents have come to trust the classic *Positive Discipline* series for its consistent, commonsense approach to child rearing. Now you can use this philosophy as a foundation for fostering cooperation, problem-solving skills and mutual respect in the classroom. Instead of controlling behavior, you can be teaching; instead of confronting apathy, you will enjoy motivated, eager students! Inside, you'll discover how to:

· Create a classroom climate that enhances academic learning

· Use encouragement rather than praise and rewards

· Instill valuable social skills and positive behavior through the use of class meetings

· Understand the motivation behind students' behavior instead of looking for causes

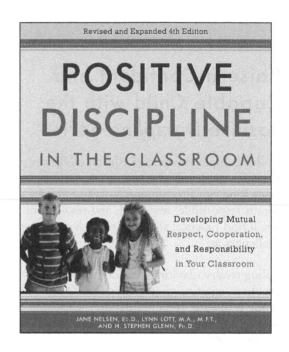

Positive Discipline in the Classroom

Raise a Confident and Capable Child with the *Positive Discipline* Series

As your child embarks on her school years, learn to positively impact her self-esteem both inside and outside the home. You'll find practical solutions for how to:

· Avoid the power struggles that often come with mastering sleeping, eating, and potty training

· Instill valuable social skills and positive behavior inside *and* outside the home by using methods that teach important life lessons

· Employ family and class meetings to tackle discipline and developmental problems

This revised and updated third edition includes information from the latest research on neurobiology, diet and exercise, gender differences and behavior, the importance of early relationships and parenting, and new approaches to parenting in the age of mass media.

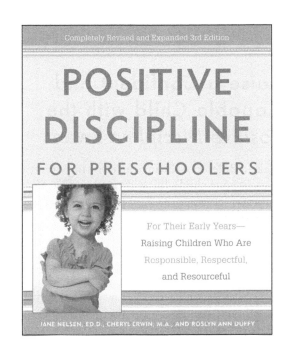

Positive Discipline for Preschoolers

Raise a Confident and Capable Child with the *Positive Discipline* Series

Make a difference during the most important years of your child's life with *Positive Discipline*'s common sense approach to parenting infants to toddlers.

Start your child out in life with the proper foundation with answers to such questions as: How do I communicate with an infant who doesn't understand words? How can I effectively teach boundaries to my toddler? Should I ever spank my child? How can I help her grow in the most loving and effective way possible?

This newly revised and updated third edition includes the latest information on neurobiology and brain development, gender differences, attachment, and the importance of early relationships to help you understand your young child's behavior.

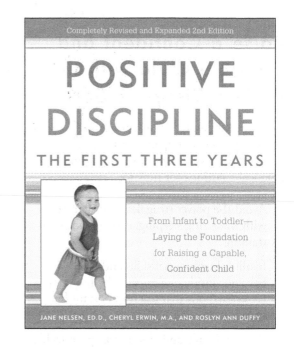

Positive Discipline: The First Three Years

A Positive, Proven Approach to Single Parenting!

In this completely revised and updated edition of *Positive Discipline for Single Parents,* you'll learn how to succeed as a single parent in the most important job of your life: raising a child who is responsible, respectful, and resourceful.

Inside this reassuring book, you'll discover how to:

· Identify potential problems and develop skills to prevent and solve them

· Create a respectful co-parenting relationship with your former spouse

· Use non-punitive methods to help your children make wise decisions about their behavior

· How to do a job alone that was meant for two people

Positive Discipline for Single Parents

Positive Parenting for Those Important Teen Years

Adolescence is a time of great stress and turmoil—not only for kids going through it, but for their parents, as well. This revised edition of *Positive Discipline for Teenagers* shows you how you can achieve greater understanding and communication with your adolescents. to make the transition to adulthood as smooth as possible. Inside, you'll:

· Grow to understand the areas in which your teen most needs your support

· Learn how to get to know who your teen really is

· Discover how to develop sound judgment without being judgmental

· Learn to use follow-through—the only surefire way to get chores done

Positive Discipline for Teenagers